The Locust Years

The Locust Years

Jacqui Williams

with David Porter

HODDER AND STOUGHTON
LONDON SYDNEY AUCKLAND TORONTO

British Library Cataloguing in Publication Data

Williams, Jacqui
  The locust years.
  1. Unification Church.
  I. Title   II. Porter, David, *1945–*
289.9   BX9750.S44

  ISBN 0 340 41069 8

*Hodder and Stoughton Editorial Office: 47 Bedford Square,
London WC1B 3DP.*

To Mum and Dad
and all those who prayed

'I will repay you for the years
the locusts have eaten ... Then
you will know that I am in
Israel, that I am the Lord your
God, and that there is no other'
(Joel 2:25, 27).

The facts recorded in this book are true to the best of my knowledge, and the opinions expressed are honestly held.

Jacqui Williams

In working with Jacqui on her book, I have been helped by a great many people and organisations. I would like to thank especially John Allan, who placed his considerable knowledge of the Unification Church at my disposal, and loaned me several important documents.

Neither he nor any other advisers, of course, should be held responsible for the opinions or presentation of the facts in the book.

David Porter

CONTENTS

1 SAN FRANCISCO

San Francisco: city (1970 pop. 715,674), co-extensive
with San Francisco co., W Calif., on the tip of a peninsula
between the Pacific Ocean and San Francisco Bay, which
are connected by the strait known as the Golden Gate ....
San Francisco is one of the most gracious and picturesque
cities in the country.

[*The International Geographic Encyclopaedia and Atlas,*
Macmillan Press, 1979.]

'I am the Messiah,' he said calmly. 'I'm God's chosen
messenger for this age.'

I edged nearer Sally. Nobody else was taking any notice.
The stranger stared at us domineeringly.

'The whole world's coming under judgment, man.' He
twitched his enormous black cape. He seemed slightly mad.
A black man in his mid-forties, he was quite good-looking,
with close-cropped curly hair. Inconsequentially, I noticed
that his shoes were expensive white ones, patent leather with
gold bars.

'Judgment, tha's what it is. I'm God's *special* son, right.
The Messiah.'

The flamboyant stranger was standing, leaning over us.
He'd picked us out, we were sitting on our own; easy targets
for his rational, unnerving tirade. I was nineteen years old
and 8,000 miles from home, and I was feeling very vulnerable indeed.

The benches in the Greyhound bus station were plastic,

screwed immovably on to a metal frame. The only way out, short of climbing over them, was to slide the length of the row, clambering over the other passengers who were sitting calmly watching our embarrassment. The four of us huddled closer together. The self-styled Messiah contemplated us bleakly. 'Gonna save the world,' he remarked. His speech was slightly slurred.

We sat meekly as he harangued us in measured tones; Graham, Roz, Sally and myself. I noticed resentfully that Graham and Roz were suppressing hysterical laughter. It was just like them. They had each other, and they could see the funny side of anything. They probably hadn't even considered the possibility that this guy could be dangerous. I glanced at Sally. She was gazing thoughtfully at the stranger.

Sally and I were the quiet ones. She was a good-humoured girl, round and jolly, who'd come to America purely because she wanted to work with children. She was scrupulously honest, and had a strong sense of personal responsibility. I felt safe with Sally. I always had the feeling that Roz and Graham might suddenly decide to go off on their own, but I knew that she wouldn't. I didn't want to be left on my own. Sally was a friend, somebody I could trust. And she had a wonderful sense of humour.

Not that either of us was finding much to laugh at in San Francisco bus station at that particular moment. We sat in embarrassed silence, hoping that the man would take the hint and go away. We had several hours to wait for our coach.

'Well?'

He swayed towards me, his eyes glittering. I stared back. 'So I need money, a heap of money, got a lot to do. How about it?'

Sally nudged me. 'He's asking for money. What do we *do*?'

I looked around anxiously. Roz and Graham were absorbed in conversation on the next bench. Suddenly, with relief, I saw two police officers approaching.

'OK, move along now.' They were solid, reassuring. The man rose with a contemptuous smile and swept off without a backward glance at us. The police smiled thinly, nodded and carried on patrolling.

The incident spoiled San Francisco for me, even blighting the memory of the previous day when we'd gone to the Fisherman's Wharf, an artists' quarter in the city.

I'd enjoyed seeing the Wharf, which was full of tiny shops and stalls selling art and craft products, and it was crowded with local people out shopping. I'd explored it all thoroughly and could have spent hours there. At Camp Walden I had been one of the camp counsellors responsible for teaching pottery, weaving and swimming.

The camp was near Cheboygan in northern Michigan, on the banks of Lake Huron, not far from the Canadian border. It was surrounded by tall pine trees and the wide waters of the lake. Around the camp site were cabins, each housing eight campers and their counsellor.

It was a very wealthy camp. The craft centre possessed ten electric pottery wheels. Most English colleges that I'd heard of had a couple of kick wheels if they were lucky. The ten splendid machines at Camp Walden were typical of the money that had been lavished on the camp.

The campers were the children of wealthy Jewish families, chiefly from Detroit. Those of us who were English had quite a dose of culture-shock. It wasn't just the fact that the wealthy children's table manners were atrocious. Having had two years' teacher training I had had quite a lot to do with children, but I was unprepared for the self-assertiveness and often brash independence that had been instilled in these rich youngsters from an early age. They were an odd mixture of apparent physical maturity and real emotional insecurity.

The English counsellors formed a natural grouping within the camp, and when it came to an end we decided to stay

together and see some of America. I had very little money –
the camp hadn't paid a great deal. But I had enough for a
Greyhound ticket. That entitled me to travel wherever I
liked in the United States for a limited period without
further cost.

Greyhound buses are notorious. I'd heard from lots of
people about how uncomfortable they were supposed to
be for travelling on long journeys, and though I'd travelled on them short distances to the camp, I was rather
apprehensive about committing myself to relying solely
on Greyhound buses for travel. But in fact I didn't find
them too bad. They were quite well fitted out with loos and
other facilities, and the seats weren't too uncomfortable;
and – most important of all – if you travelled on the night
coaches, you didn't see much of the scenery but you got a
night's sleep without having to check in at a hotel. In my
brand-new, expensive rucksack that I'd brought from
England and which was my only luggage, I'd packed a
sleeping bag.

We were an oddly assorted group. Roz was in her early
twenties and was vivacious, willing to try anything. She was
looking for a good time. She'd had a couple of boyfriends
during the camp, and had adroitly avoided getting too
involved with either of them. Graham had been to a public
school and was clever and amusing. He was a striking-
looking person, gaunt face framing watery, glazed eyes. He
ate very little but drank tea incessantly. He and Roz formed
a natural pair, and Sally and I had a lot in common.

We travelled thousands of miles by coach. From Detroit
we went right through the corn country of the Mid-West,
through Illinois and Kansas and on to the Grand Canyon.
We had a day out in Denver, and went up into the mountains
where there was a natural amphitheatre. We listened to a
rock concert there. Later, travelling by night through the
Nevada desert, we saw the lights of of Las Vegas miles ahead
lighting up the sky; and from Vegas we went on to San

Francisco where we encountered the man who thought he was God.

Changing from coach to coach, travelling at night and sightseeing by day, we visited Los Angeles, the Grand Canyon, San Diego, Las Vegas and eventually, on the very borders of Mexico, El Paso.

In many ways it was the most exciting time of my life. Even the lack of money added a sparkle to the adventure. I lived off muesli most of the time, adding fresh fruit as and when I could. Roz and Graham were exhilarating companions, Sally was a good friend, and I was seeing more of America than I would ever have thought possible in one relatively short trip.

But I was restless inside. I had been, ever since the first days in the camp. Even though I'd often detested the wealthy Detroit kids, with their awful manners and brash self-assurance, I'd envied them. They had all the hallmarks of the close social structures of Reformed Judaism, down to the gold necklaces which many of them wore, with Star of David pendants, and the elaborate dental braces which indicated that their parents were wealthy enough to afford expensive dental care.

They belonged to their group, and I was an outsider. Being English made it worse, but there was more to it than that. I was envious of that mystique of belonging, that didn't depend so much on who you were as a person but what you were born into. I envied the acceptance that membership of such a group guaranteed.

I'd left England as a Christian, but without a Christian family, either in the usual sense or the wider one. I didn't have a Christian peer group – most of the people I knew were either a lot older or a lot younger than me. My Christianity was very much a matter of 'Thou shalt nots', and I was very unsure in the world of dating and drinking and all the other things that were going on in the camp. There was even marijuana circulating among the counsellors.

I longed for a Christianity that wasn't just an intellectual exercise or moral system, but one which gave me a framework within which to live and a family to belong to.

I felt like a loner, on the fringe of things. I wanted to be part of a group. I was an extremely moral person looking for an environment in which to be moral.

At El Paso we spent a few days sightseeing. We crossed the border into Mexico and bought souvenirs – I found a nice rug for my parents.

We discussed what to do next. Our flights home were from John F. Kennedy airport in New York, and the others planned to go there by way of Florida and the South-East, going up the East Coast to New York.

But I had different plans. I still wanted to visit a Christian community. I thought I would find one on the West Coast; that was where things seemed to be happening. And on the West Coast, San Francisco was the city where the most interesting things seemed to be going on.

When I announced this to my companions they tried to make me change my mind.

'You're crazy!' they argued. 'You'll be on your own when we leave. America's not any sort of a place to travel round on your own.'

'And San Francisco!' added Roz. 'That's where that weirdo was – the guy who said he was the Messiah – remember?'

She was right. San Francisco had been a let-down. But last time, I'd been a sightseer. Now it was different. I had a reason for travelling, something to find at the end of it. It wouldn't be the same.

Despite their best efforts I refused to change my mind. Soon we were saying our goodbyes, and I waved them off as the Florida coach trundled out of the bus station and out of sight.

Not long afterwards I was on my own coach, bound for

San Diego, a pleasant and prosperous city where I changed to another coach that took me to San Francisco.

I arrived on a Friday. By the time the coach got there I had changed my mind about making San Francisco my base. In England I'd known a Barney Coombes who'd been in a charismatic church in Basingstoke and was now involved in some sort of a Christian community project in Vancouver, Canada. Now, reviewing my options, I remembered him. The link with England was an attraction. I decided to go to Canada and visit the community.

The bus station at San Francisco was just as I remembered it – the rows of plastic seats, rubbish and scraps of paper blowing about, and passengers like myself, waiting in an in-between limbo for their next coach.

I dumped my rucksack on a bench and glanced round, half-expecting a visionary in a black cloak and white shoes to appear with a slurred message of world salvation. Nobody paid any attention to me. It felt curiously lonely without my travelling companions. There was a lot to be said for being bored together.

On a wall near by, a timetable was displayed. I went across to check the coach schedules. I would have to go to Seattle to catch the first connection.

'Hi!'

I turned to find a young man in his early twenties standing at my side. He looked cool and comfortable in blue slacks and a checked shirt open at the neck.

'Excuse me,' he said pleasantly, 'did you just get off the coach from San Diego?'

'Yes.'

'Do you happen to know whether Mary was on it?'

I thought for a moment, taken aback by his question. He seemed to think I knew her. I scratched my head. 'I don't think so. What does she look like?'

'Oh – fair-skinned, blonde, quite short. About twenty-one.'

'No,' I volunteered. 'I don't think there was anybody like that on the bus.' I had been sitting on my own at the front. It was the best place from which to watch the scenery changing. The only other passengers I remembered seeing on the coach had been a couple of older people.

He shrugged. 'Doesn't matter. She'll make her own way, I guess.' He scanned the timetable. 'Where are you headed for?'

'Seattle.'

'Quite some time to wait. Want some coffee?'

I looked at him appraisingly. He seemed extremely clean-cut, friendly, and straightforward; an attractive person to whom I warmed immediately. My initial reserve began to thaw. Travelling on my own had already made me somewhat cautious about people, and in San Francisco I was especially so, with the memory very fresh in my mind of the lunatic visionary I had encountered last time. But I was impressed by this man. He seemed all right.

Over coffee we got into conversation. I learned that his name was Sam. 'Why are you going to Seattle?' he asked. I told him of my plans to go to Vancouver. 'To visit a Christian community,' I explained.

Sam looked up. 'That's interesting,' he commented. 'I live in a Christian community, right here in San Francisco.'

I began to bombard him with questions. 'Look,' he suggested, 'I'm here with a few friends. Tonight we're having an open evening. We invite folk in to explain what we're about, why we live in community, and what the thinking is behind it.'

It sounded very attractive indeed, and I fancied the idea of spending some time indoors in pleasant company. The thought of the long ride up to Vancouver wasn't at all attractive, and I wasn't even sure where the community was up there.

So when Sam asked me if I'd like to go to the open evening, I accepted immediately. 'We'll just wait for the others,' he said, and as we talked people began to join us. It was about four o'clock. They seemed very pleasant people, mostly of my own age or a little older, though two women were in their mid-thirties. I was struck by how fresh and sun-tanned they all were.

Sam introduced me to everybody, and then led the way to a large station-wagon. We climbed aboard, and were soon driving through the city. San Francisco is built on hills, and the house we arrived at – a beautiful pale-blue wood-clad building up on Hearst Street – looked down one of its prosperous, tree-lined avenues.

The main living room was spacious, with wide bay windows overlooking the avenue. There were quite a few people in the room when we arrived. 'Let's sit down,' said Sam. 'Supper will be ready soon.'

Others came in, in ones and twos. Somebody produced a guitar. The girl sitting next to me reached for my hand. Linked in a large circle, we all sang 'Annie's Song', a John Denver composition that was very popular then.

I loved it when we all held hands and sang that song. Not that the song itself meant anything to me; it was the feeling of acceptance, of being part of a group. This was part of what I had been looking for. A warm, agreeable feeling began to grow inside me.

Supper was an enormous tureen of spiral pasta with a tomato sauce, and its appearance was greeted with hilarity by many present, who seemed to know the cook well.

'Carlotta! This your special sauce?'

'Wow, that smells real good!'

'None for me, Carlotta, I'm driving ....'

My neighbour whispered in my ear. 'Carlotta's ragout sauce is famous. She always puts at least half a bottle of red wine in.'

It was a delicious meal. It was particularly interesting to me, as I was a vegetarian. I mentioned to them when I arrived that I didn't eat meat, so I was very pleased when I saw the food that was provided.

During the meal, various people got up and contributed entertainment of various kinds – songs, jokes, and other offerings. I was impressed by the fact that all the humour was clean. At the camp and on the road I'd heard many filthy jokes and crude songs; here it was different, without being sanctimonious. It had been a long time since I had warmed to a group of people as I was warming to these.

Afterwards we all relaxed. I chatted to Sam. He didn't try to introduce me to everybody in the room, but simply talked about generalities – telling me, for example, that all the vegetables in the meal we had just eaten had been grown by the community on a farm they ran. Looking round the room I could see one or two others who were obviously visitors and were similarly relaxing.

After a while, everybody began to move to one end of the large room, and a pair of sliding partition doors were drawn across to make a smaller room. From behind the partition I could hear the cheerful noise of supper dishes being collected.

Then Dr Moses Durst, who had been pointed out to me by Sam as the leader of the group, rose to his feet. He was a stocky, dark-haired man with a New York Jewish accent, and he had a humorous twinkle in his eye.

Sam had told me that Dr Durst was a professor of English literature at a local university. His students must have enjoyed their studies. He was an entertaining and humorous speaker, and though his talk covered a great deal of ground it didn't seem heavy listening at all.

People, he said, no longer cared for one another. Man was essentially selfish, and the result was a broken world. The reason why this community existed, he explained, was to counter that by living a shared life. 'There are enough resources in the world for everyone,' argued Dr Durst. 'Some people have to be aware of that and live accordingly.'

When he finished I realised that there had been no religious content at all. It had all been in terms of good and evil, but there was nothing in it that you could have called a religious message.

I asked Sam about it. 'I thought you said this was a Christian community? He didn't mention God.'

'Well,' said Sam thoughtfully, 'a lot of people come here who are in one kind of need or another, and they've never thought about the real issues. They might be on drugs, or on the road, or just drifting through life. So what we really try to do is to start by talking about what we do, our food distribution programmes for example. Then we try to build on that and explain about man's responsibility to mankind, and about evil.'

The food distribution programme, I had already learned from Sam, meant that if the local farms produced more food than was needed or could be sold, the surplus was collected by the community and distributed to the poor in San Francisco.

Later slides were shown of the community's own farm – Boonville – showing the activities that went on there, the farming and the food production; and they showed slides of places where they gave lectures like the one I had heard that night. I was becoming more and more excited by all that I was hearing. Boonville sounded fascinating. In the mornings and evenings there were workshops and seminars, and in the afternoons everybody worked on the land, picking courgettes, tomatoes and sweetcorn, for example.

But it cost thirty dollars to go there.

I wanted to go very much, and I was sure that I wouldn't be able to as I was terribly short of money. I was living off very little, and thirty dollars seemed a great deal to spend if I was going to go back to New York via Vancouver.

'I just can't afford it,' I confessed to Sam.

'Well,' he said comfortably, 'why not just come along?'

'What do you mean?'

'We could sponsor you. Don't worry about the money. Some people visit Boonville who can't afford it. Money's not the most important thing.'

So it was decided. As it was a Friday, a group was going up to Boonville for the weekend. We travelled in a bright yellow school bus which the group owned. On the way we sang songs. I sang some Christian songs which I knew, and they seemed to go down very well with everybody.

Night fell, and we could no longer see outside the windows. Inside the bus, we were a close group, cheerful and together. I was feeling very happy.

2 BOONVILLE

The experience is properly called a workshop. The Divine Principle without the example of people living it out would not have been as moving.

[Daniel Davies recalling a Unification Church weekend workshop in New York in Richard Quebedeaux and Rodney Sawatsky (eds), *Evangelical-Unification Dialogue*, 1979.]

The bus growled through its gears and swayed round a bend in the highway. I leaned sideways on the hard plastic seat. Most of the other people in the bus were asleep, curled awkwardly into rounded, shadowed humps. The interior lights had been switched off. The driver and a companion in the front cab, their faces briefly lit by the headlights of passing cars, occasionally made conversation. The driver's eyes were fixed on the road.

I was too excited to sleep. Under my breath I hummed phrases from the songs I'd been singing half an hour before. I'd been singing partly to stay awake – I didn't want to miss any of this new experience. I'd picked up a guitar and sung some Christian choruses. To my surprise people had come and sat near me to listen. I haven't got a particularly strong singing voice, and the fact that I felt relaxed enough to perform in public was just one more remarkable thing out of many that had happened since I met Sam at the bus station.

But now everybody round me was asleep. Staring at the blackness through the window, half dozing, half alert, I lost track of time. Hours went by. We were steadily going uphill. Occasionally I could see lights far below in the valleys.

The bus toiled up a steep track and pulled noisily to a stop. I rubbed my eyes and stretched. All around me, the others were waking up in confusion and yawning.

We stumbled to the door and clambered down. Outside it was pitch black, and cold with the thin chill of night in the hills. I stamped my feet discreetly in an attempt to get the circulation back. A short distance away, I could see lighted windows.

Our hosts sorted us into males and females. I went with the rest of the women, stumbling along the unfamiliar ground. We were shown into a large room. Rows of foam mattresses were laid on the floor. Everybody was bleary-eyed. In a matter of minutes, we were all fast asleep.

The morning sun was hot on my face as I woke up. I had a good look round the room. It was clean and sparse, empty except for the sleeping bodies. The bathroom was attractively tiled and sparkling clean. After several nights on a coach it was nice to have a proper wash.

I went outdoors into a bright hot morning and gasped with pleasure. All around, hills shimmered in haze. The fields were parched with the heat of summer, and the grass was long and scorched a rich, golden yellow. Vegetable plots sloped away into the distance.

The farm consisted of several wooden buildings. Other girls were emerging from the one in which I had slept, and some boys began to appear from what looked like an old chicken-shed turned into a dormitory. Near by, some people were setting out breakfast things. I wandered over.

'Hi!' A girl looked up as I approached, and gave me a friendly smile.

'Hello,' I smiled back. 'I'm Jacqui.'

'Well, Jacqui, welcome to Boonville. Did you sleep?'

'I certainly did,' I assured her. She grinned.

'I'm not surprised. It's a long drive out here.'

I picked up some plates and began to help.

We had oatmeal for breakfast, with chunks of fresh fruit. It was washed down with orange juice mixed with the very thick reconstituted American milk I'd got used to during the summer. The food was delicious, and the sharply-sweet taste of the drink wasn't unpleasant.

We sat in a semi-circle and talked and talked. Sam sat with me. I found it very easy to talk to him. For one thing, he seemed genuinely interested – in me, in my background, in what I had been doing in America that summer, and in what had brought me back to San Francisco. Though he asked lots of questions, he didn't seem inquisitive. I noticed that those of the group whom I knew to be newcomers like myself were each being looked after just as I was.

A woman in her mid-thirties, Becky, appeared to be the leader. She was very petite, with a wonderful laugh and a talent for making people feel welcome. She and Sam occasionally called out comments to each other. They were clearly old friends, and Sam was some sort of a leader in this group.

Afterwards we sat for a while digesting our breakfast and letting the sun beat down on our backs. Eventually Becky clapped her hands:

'OK, everybody!'

We all got to our feet. Sam indicated a large building. 'Lecture,' he informed me laconically. We walked together into the building, which housed rows of chairs, a blackboard and some simple decorations.

The lecture was similar to the one I had heard in San Francisco. It was given by Sandy, who had been at breakfast and was a leader of the community. She had been one of the people for whom Sam had been waiting at the bus station, and she had come out with us in the school bus.

I listened intently to what Sandy had to say. I agreed with her analysis of the state of the world; as a Christian I certainly accepted that man was in a great deal of trouble. Also, there was more identifiable Christian content in the lecture than there had been in Dr Durst's talk, and I smiled knowledgeably to myself. *There are people here*, I thought, *who don't know what they're letting themselves in for!*

After the lecture we were organised into groups for discussion; then lunch, which was delicious; and in the afternoon we were allocated tasks in the fields – I picked zucchini. Even that labour was satisfying, toiling in the fields breathing fresh air and occasionally pausing to wonder at the scenery.

In the evening we had almost a barbecue – we took food up to the top of one of the hills, and made a huge fire. We all sat round in the firelight. Somebody passed copies of a song book round – *The Boonville Songbook*. Flipping through mine, I noticed several names I knew already – John Denver, Bob Dylan, old Woodstock songs and others. We sang, and various people got up and contributed items of entertainment. I sat quietly, enjoying everything, feeling amazingly peaceful.

In some ways it was a little bit like the camp I had left in Cheboygan; the same orderly sequence of tasks and activities, the same teaching emphasis, the same semi-regimentation. But in so many ways it was quite different. There, it had been centred on the children's needs and demands. Here, it was as if everybody was working for one another, and there was a real commitment between the members of the community. I quickly noticed, for example, that they referred to one another as 'Brothers' and 'Sisters', and it seemed that the terms really meant something.

As the weekend progressed, so did my interest in the community. There was a much more defined biblical background at Boonville; though they didn't have Bible studies as such, it was mentioned constantly and Bible passages were explained at length. There was also discussion of other religions, and I found some of the insights quite helpful; for example, symbols from Eastern philosophy were used as illustrations of the notion of opposites.

There was no doubt about it, Boonville met a number of needs that I wanted satisfied. There was a sense of purpose about the place, a feeling that there was truth waiting to be discovered; the people were kind and committed to one another; it was biblically orientated; there was plenty to occupy my mind; and I was enjoying the opportunity to work out of doors and eat good, wholesome food, after weeks of junk meals and near-starvation brought about by rigorous economies.

Curiously, the group's strong community identity became almost a threat. They had such a clear sense of who they were and what they were about; was I welcome within it, I wondered? Did I fit?

It had been described as a 'weekend workshop', and as Monday loomed I felt wretched. It was like being on a roundabout at a fairground, when you feel the machine slowing down and you wonder how long you'll be allowed to stay on the ride; sooner or later your money is going to run out.

How long, I wondered, would the goodwill last? After all, I was only there by grace and favour – I hadn't paid my thirty dollars.

Perhaps because of these forebodings, I joined in everything that was going on during the weekend. And I prayed, all the time; constantly thanking God for bringing me to this place, and desperately hoping that by some miracle I would be able to stay.

It seemed that all weekend I was with people, either in group activities like preparing a meal or working in the fields, when somebody from the community always struck up a conversation; or in a group listening to a lecture with about thirty others. It was a packed schedule. There was no time to be alone; even at night, when I crawled thankfully into my sleeping bag, my extreme (though by no means unpleasant) tiredness prevented too close an analysis of the day's events. Sam was constantly at my side, anticipating my every need and always ready to answer my questions. It was a kind of security. After travelling on my own without a clear goal, now I was in a community, where I knew exactly what was going to happen every moment of the day.

I knew that my original plan to go to Vancouver had become almost irrelevant. My main preoccupation, as Sunday evening approached, was: how on earth was I going to stay with these people? Suddenly it was the most important question in the world.

That evening I was sitting with Sam at supper, talking about something fairly trivial, when Becky came over to us and sat down, arranging herself in such a way that Sam's back and her own formed a small barrier between me and the others. She smiled cheerfully:

'Having a good time, Jacqui?'

'Oh, yes!' I exclaimed. Sam laughed.

'We sure talked a lot,' he said. 'Didn't waste a minute since Friday night!'

Becky laughed. I grinned ruefully.

'I really am grateful to you for letting me come,' I said. 'Especially as I couldn't afford it. You've been very kind. Thank you.'

Becky looked at me very directly, straight in the eyes. 'Have you learned a little bit about us?'

'Yes, I think so,' I said, remembering the hours of lectures, the discussions, and the long conversations with Sam. It seemed an age since Friday, when I had met these people for the first time, but I had only been at Boonville for two days. In those two days, what had I learned? In one sense, very little indeed. I'd been told that the name of the community was the Creative Community Project, but I knew hardly anything about its history or its organisation. I'd heard many hours of lectures, but had found it hard to fit what I'd heard into my previous experience, though I agreed with most of what had been said and was willing to suspend judgment on the rest until I'd had a chance to think about it all. And I'd worked hard, talked hard, and generally had a wonderful time.

Becky was watching me carefully. She was more serious than I had seen her that weekend. The hearty, booming laugh wasn't in evidence. She chose her words cautiously, as if feeling her way forward in the conversation.

'What will you do now, Jacqui?'

I thought for a moment, and then said honestly, 'I don't know.'

Sam leaned forward. 'I think that you've obviously understood the kind of things we've been talking about this weekend. Probably more than the rest.'

I nodded soberly. It was true. I had understood; I'd felt at home, in a strange kind of way. And I wasn't worried by the fact that the leaders weren't stressing the biblical basis of the community's teaching, because most of the newcomers had clearly had little or no spiritual experience before. Also, it was apparent that some of the visitors who had particularly weird and far-out lifestyles had met with prejudice from extreme fundamentalist Christian groups, and therefore the leaders were reticent in showing their hand too soon.

'Yes,' I agreed. 'I see what you mean.'

Sam beamed. 'Right!' he said. 'But you know, you've only scratched the surface. Sure, we covered the basics. How mankind is selfish and God needs to restore the world. Where history's going. What God thinks of how man is handling things. But that's just the beginning.'

Behind Sam and Becky I could see the others getting up from supper and moving away. Sam and Becky made no move. We remained seated, the remains of our meal stacked between us. Fragments of intense conversations wafted back to us on the dusky air. There was a feeling of winding down, of the weekend coming to a close.

'Do you have any place to go, Jacqui?' Becky's voice was

neutral, but as I began to wonder where the conversation was leading, I felt a growing excitement.

'Well – I thought, Vancouver ....'

But even as I was saying the words I knew that I had finally decided not to go to Vancouver.

Sam cleared his throat. 'We have a place in Santa Rosa, a couple of hours' drive from here. Camp K. You'd be welcome to go on to there. It's a place where people can take things further, discuss more, hear more lectures, get in deeper.' He smiled again, a comfortable, conspiratorial smile. 'Kind of graduate school,' he added.

Once again I was astonished by the fact that I was being accepted and that these people were interested in me. *Thank you, Lord*, I thought. Surely it was a gift from him. After all, I'd come looking for a Christian community, and the others had stumbled into it by accident. So I'd had a head start; what some of the others had probably viewed as a complex and unavoidable series of lectures, I'd welcomed and found stimulating. Sam and Becky's invitation to Camp K was just what I most wanted.

A worrying thought suddenly crossed my mind.

'But I can't go,' I said flatly, my suppressed excitement evaporating. 'I can't afford it. I didn't even have thirty dollars to come here. I've been living on three dollars a day. My money's almost finished.'

Becky was sympathetic. 'Well, we really do like people to contribute something towards their keep, but as you know from this weekend, we don't make it an absolute condition. Is there no way you could get some more money?'

I made my mind up. 'I'll contact my parents and ask them to bank-wire me some money.' It was a simple procedure; I'd always had it at the back of my mind as an emergency measure.

'That's fine,' said Sam. There was a pause. I felt awkward. 'How long do people usually stay at Camp K?' I asked.

'Oh, various periods,' Becky replied. 'It depends on

what's right for them. Sometimes a few days – sometimes a few months – sometimes longer.'

I felt terribly embarrassed. Here was I, thrusting myself upon a community of people and expecting them to pay my board and lodging. Becky eyed me curiously, and deduced what I was thinking.

'Have you no money at all?' she asked, not unkindly.

'Well,' I calculated, 'I've about twenty dollars ... I'd be happy for you to have that, really I would; and when the money comes from my parents I can pay what people usually pay.'

'That's fine,' said Sam, as if anxious to move on to less embarrassing topics. But I had a brainwave.

'Look,' I said, fishing in my pocket. 'I've got this.' And I held out my Greyhound pass. 'It has to be worth something, it's got several weeks to run.'

Sam reached out and took the pass. He glanced at it and handed it to Becky. 'That's really good,' he said. 'Thank you. That's more than a donation. That's a commitment!'

When they accepted the Greyhound pass, it was as if I had been finally accepted into the community.

'We'll leave for Camp K quite early tomorrow,' said Becky. We stood up and watched the embers of the bonfire growing dull and grey. The inky night cloudbanks were piling up over the hills. We strolled to the lecture hall, catching up with the other visitors, some of whom turned and greeted us with smiles.

But I felt different now. After so long a search, a sense of acceptance and belonging was growing inside me. It was a tentative fragile beginning, and I still felt doubtful. Did they really want me? I was sure I wanted them. I wanted to be in this group and share its lifestyle. Yet gnawing at the back of my mind was the fear that I would not make the grade.

But I was going to Camp K, and Sam was coming with me! I'd made a commitment. I belonged. For how long, I didn't know; but it didn't matter. I was accepted.

3 CAMP K

The vast majority of Moonies are intelligent, idealistic young people who have joined and remain in the movement by their own choice .... not because they have been brainwashed but because they believe the Unification Church holds the key to the salvation of the world.

[Irving Hexham and Myrtle Langley, 'Cracking the Moonie Code', *Credo* (student journal of Regent College, Vancouver), September 1979.]

Of those of us who left Boonville early the next morning, some were Creative Community Project members, and a few were like myself, newcomers who had stayed on to learn more.

As the bus drove off down the track I looked back to the wooden buildings of the farm and the fields of vegetables. People were out already, picking produce. It was going to be another hot Californian day.

I was sitting in a window seat, with Sam next to me. He pointed out interesting landmarks as we drove along. There was plenty to see. On Greyhound coaches I'd become used to the American straight road system; long highways disappearing into the distance, and long monotonous vistas which hardly changed from one hour to the next. But travelling through the Californian hills to Santa Rosa was different; the roads were narrower, and wound in and out of the slopes. There was always something to see round the next bend.

It seemed hardly any time at all – though in fact we'd been travelling for about two hours – before we were turning off the main road and passing through a cantilever gate that was raised to let us through.

'Camp K,' Sam informed me.

A long driveway climbed up the hillside. As Camp K itself came into view, I realised that it was a much bigger place than Boonville. We rolled gently to a stop outside a substantial building, bigger than any at the farm, and I could see other buildings higher up the hill. They were all permanent structures, whereas at Boonville the premises had been wooden and looked temporary.

We collected our bags and were told where we would be sleeping. The girls' dormitory was like that at Boonville, very sparse and clean, in a white brick building that looked quite recently built. Bedding was stacked against the wall, leaving the floor free for cleaning. I've never been to a Girl Guides' camp, but the dormitory looked like I've always imagined one would be like.

We didn't say more than a few words to one another as we dumped our bags. We were directed almost immediately to the main hall. The room was filled with about fifty people. I felt rather out of things. As I came into the hall, Sam appeared and showed me to a seat. He had obviously been waiting for me. I was glad to see a familiar face.

'Who are all these people?' I asked Sam.

'Some are members of the community, others are people who are visiting. Most of them have been here for a while. Over there' – he pointed across the room – 'is Zack Stern, he'll be giving the lectures.' I followed his gaze. A tall, very thin man, who looked Asian, was chatting to a small group. He seemed very intense.

I surveyed the gathering. It seemed that a member of the community was accompanying each of us who were new-comers.

'What sort of lectures will they be?'

'It's kind of a progression on from Boonville,' explained Sam. 'It's a seven-day workshop. The lectures build on one another. You'll enjoy it.'

'OK, everybody!'

I looked round. Zack Stern was standing at the door. 'Welcome to Camp K,' he said formally. Let's get right into things. Will everybody please go through to the lecture room and sit down.'

The lecture room was set out very formally, with the speaker's lectern and a big blackboard at the front and rows of individual study-seats equipped with writing desks, each provided with a pad and a neatly sharpened pencil.

Zack was an excellent speaker. He quickly broke the ice and was humorous and, at the same time, impressively serious. He gave the impression that we were there to talk about things that were important.

The lecture was very similar to those at Boonville, but there was a significant change in emphasis. At the farm, there had been a concentration on social responsibility, world problems, and how to help to build a better world by serving other people. That had been the impulse behind the food distribution programme and the other activities at the farm. But here, at the very beginning of the workshop, the emphasis was on broad historical patterns and the state of the cosmos.

That didn't mean it was boring. Zack had a fund of illustrations and anecdotes, and I found the lecture riveting. Its theme – the fall of man – was one I was familiar with, but this was an entirely new angle.

There was a lively discussion after he sat down. I felt as if I were back in my old college, at the end of an intensive seminar. I grinned at Sam. 'I'm going to enjoy this!'

It didn't take me long to fit into the routine of Camp K. The place itself was very pleasant, like a retreat centre, its chalet-style buildings scattered up the hillside. Nobody ate indoors. There was a small stream, which made a shady oasis in the middle of the parched, stubbly pasture. We sat by the water in small groups, eating wholemeal bread spread with home-made peanut butter and honey and other good food.

There were recreational times; there was even a grassed basket-ball pitch at the top of the hill, where occasionally a group organised a game on the rough uneven surface. But there wasn't very much time for sport, since the lecture programme and the discussions took up most of the time. However, for those who were out of bed in time, there were daily physical exercises. I made sure that I never missed a session. In both exercises and games we were encouraged to be extremely competitive, and to lose well. We were divided into teams, and each team had to appoint its cheer-leader, who devised rousing chants and incited the team to roar them enthusiastically while playing. If one's team was losing, we were told, then it was especially important to keep chanting and to resist the temptation to fade into embarrassed silence. It was an early taste of an attitude which was later to become second nature to me.

At first, Sam sat next to me in the lectures. All the visitors had a community member sitting beside them. I found it helpful, because I could discuss things with Sam, and I enjoyed arguing with him over various points.

A day or two after I arrived, I went into the lecture room for the first lecture of the day, and sat down in my usual place. To my surprise, Sam wasn't anywhere to be seen; in his place was a girl called Amy, a member of the community whom I had seen in the dormitory.

'Where's Sam?' I asked curiously.

Amy looked vague. 'Oh, he had to go back to the city,' she said.

'Back?'

'Well, sometimes we have to move around,' said Amy. 'Sam was needed somewhere else.' My face must have looked crestfallen, for she laughed. 'Don't worry,' she said. 'I'll look after you. You can come to me if you want anything.'

Amy was a friendly, outgoing sort of person, but I found her difficult to get on with. There wasn't the same easy-going relationship I had had with Sam. She was slightly overbearing, and sometimes very annoying.

She stayed with me everywhere I went. The first night after Sam left, Amy moved her sleeping bag next to mine. At meal times she sat with me. When I went for a stroll on the hill between lectures, she would appear just as I was leaving: 'Out for a walk? Great, I'll string along.'

I realised that Sam had been ever-present too, but in a much more unobtrusive way. When I needed to go to the loo, for instance, Sam always seemed to be waiting when I emerged from the bathroom. I didn't think much about this – we were usually deep in conversation beforehand, and it was natural for him to hang around waiting for me so we could continue talking. But the first time I needed to go to the loo after Sam left, Amy came into the bathroom with me, and calmly waited outside the cubicle, talking cheerfully until I'd finished.

There was a strong sense of structure about Camp K, a feeling that every minute was planned. There was an intense sense of direction and motivation, and it all ran smoothly considering that there were about fifty visitors to be fed, housed and organised into the lecture schedule. The wonder was that the leaders succeeded in maintaining a firm hold of the situation while at the same time being popular and well-liked.

The two most prominent leaders were Zack Stern and a woman called Jessica whom I liked very much. She was quite a bit older than me, an educational psychologist, and very eloquent. She gave occasional lectures, but her main contri-bution was in the small discussion groups. She struck me as a very caring person.

The longer I stayed at Camp K the more I felt that I had found at last the environment I had been looking for. As a Christian I had always been aware of a tension within myself; I wanted very much not to compromise what I had learned from the Bible, but living in the world meant that all the time one was faced with choices. There were opportunities on every side to live immorally – and yet, I couldn't help thinking that though it was right to live morally it did mean that you were losing more than you were gaining.

At college I became adept at walking a spiritual tightrope; not allowing myself to become the sort of person whom nobody ever invited to parties or discos, but at the same time, never allowing myself to go to too many of them, and always somehow keeping a distance between myself and the male rugby-club set that dominated our college. I just didn't want to close all the doors.

At Camp K, perhaps because I'd given them my money and my Greyhound pass, I felt as if I belonged. And it was within the biblical framework, because the community was a Christian community; yet it was different, because these people had a different approach from any Christian teaching I had yet heard. I wrote to my parents and enthused over my good fortune. I also asked them to bank-wire me some money urgently.

The lectures at Camp K were a good example of the different approach. They began with an exposition of the fall of man, and a discussion of the role of Adam and Eve. Then God's purpose was traced throughout history, leading up to the life of John the Baptist and Jesus.

The original purpose of God for man, Zack explained, was that he should be fruitful and multiply. His plan was for a perfect individual, within a perfect family. Zack drew out example after example, from the Bible and from modern life, of the imperfection of human marriages and the ideal which God longed for.

The next stage of the argument took some grappling with, but Zack was a very good lecturer and Sam and Amy discussed it with me at length. In essence, said Zack, Jesus's mission has not been properly understood until it is viewed from the perspective of God's plan for mankind. Jesus was the perfect man; therefore his destiny was to form a perfect family. His death on the cross, explained Zack, was not what God had originally wanted. It was never part of his plan. It was a second-best.

I grappled with these new ideas. They made sense, but they didn't fit in with my previous understanding. Didn't Jesus come to save the world? Wasn't the cross the whole reason why he came? And if so, didn't that mean that his work was a triumph, not a failure?

'I think the problem's partly your evangelical background,' said Amy. I was immediately on the defensive, because she didn't say it particularly sensitively. But as she continued she did make sense:

'You see, Jacqui, you're probably hung up on particular ways of saying things. You think that if something isn't spelt out in a formula that you're familiar with, then it's suspect. But try to cut loose from that. What you're hearing here is a whole new way of looking at the Bible. D'you think it's reasonable to imagine that everything that can be said about Scripture has been said?'

I shook my head and laughed. 'No, you're right.'

So I made a conscious effort to open my mind up to new ways of looking at things. 'Look,' said Amy, 'the New Testament reinterprets the Old Testament, right? Prophecies, things like that, only make sense when you go into the New Testament.'

'Right,' I nodded.

'Well, OK then, think of what you're learning now as reinterpreting the New Testament. That figures, doesn't it?'

'Yes,' I said thoughtfully. 'I think it does . . .'

There were some people in the group who were very negative all week. They disliked the community, they objected to being so tightly organised, they argued after lectures. Whatever had brought them to Camp K in the first place, they had lost their enthusiasm very rapidly. The leaders used to say that they were 'negging out', and they caused real problems in the Camp.

Others were apathetic. They couldn't care less about the lectures, Camp K hadn't turned out the way they imagined it would, and they just didn't want to know. And that also caused problems, because a lot of groundwork had to be gone over for their benefit, covering things like moral absolutes, which they didn't want to go along with.

As the week progressed I found myself trying to encourage the apathetic and reason with the 'neggers-out'. Because I believed in God and the Bible, and had a basis for believing that there were such things as moral absolutes, I could see that although I had some problems with what was being taught at Camp K, it was much more logical than what the critics were saying. So I found myself taking the side of the community more and more.

My own interest was increasing all the time, and everything began to take shape when I listened later in the week to a lecture on the Lord of the Second Advent. The lecture revolved around Jesus's return, and what form it would take. I was familiar with various schemes of prophetic timetable, and I listened with interest as Zack made out a well-argued, convincing case for the coming of the Lord of the Second Advent in – the 1920s.

I had been following the argument carefully, making painstaking notes, and it took a little while for the implications to sink in. If the argument was correct, then the Lord of the Second Advent was already on earth!

Zack pressed the point home. The event had taken place, and God was redeeming the world in a new way through that means. And the Messiah was going to appear in the world just as Jesus did at first – an incarnate man, walking the earth.

And if *that* were the case, then we might be about to see the fulfilment of God's original plan in all its glory; the perfect man, in a perfect marriage, raising perfect children.

I realised that I'd never thought very much about what Jesus's return would be like, nor had I really considered what he would do when he came back. I knew that he would reign on a renewed earth and that Christians would 'reign with him' – but what did that mean in practice? I listened carefully, with a growing excitement, and resolved to find out more.

My resolve was satisfied on the last night of lectures, Saturday night. We were told that it was to be about the growth of the movement of which the community was part, and I was very much looking forward to hearing it. I still knew very little about the community's background, apart from the fact that they had a distinctive view of the Bible, that they had a strong sense of social responsibility, and that there seemed to be a large number of Asians involved.

Zack began by telling us the story of the 'Inside Belly Church' that began in the early years of this century in Korea. The name was peculiar but appropriate. A Korean woman had been told in a vision that Jesus was going to come again from the womb of a woman. She actually experienced a kind of phantom pregnancy, but bore no child; clearly the prophecy referred to someone else. And the prophetic vision went on to tell the woman that clothes and food should be made ready for the Son of God, and that by so doing the foundations would be laid for the Messiah to be born.

So the woman and her neighbours made a new set of clothes, prepared food every day, and offered it on an altar.

Then, Zack went on, there was a Presbyterian farming family in Korea, and in 1920 they had a son called Sun

Myung Moon, a boy of exceptional piety and meditation. When he was sixteen years old, while praying on a mountainside, he had a revelation from God that he had been chosen for a great task. Jesus himself, claimed Moon, had appeared to him. In the years that followed there were further visions and revelations, culminating in a crucial encounter in 1945 in which Jesus gave him a commission to go out into the world and reveal what had been taught him.

Zack related anecdotes about the young Sun Myung Moon – how he spent four days and four nights chasing a stoat, never giving up until he caught it; how he was bullied as a child, and never fought back; how he was conspicuous by his moral behaviour, and nobody could point an accusing finger at him.

From that beginning in Korea had grown up the Unification Church; the community was part of it, it was a world-wide movement, and the lectures we had been hearing were based on a book of Sun Myung Moon's teachings called *Divine Principle*.

And Sun Myung Moon himself? He was married, and had a family. In the Unification Church Mr and Mrs Moon were called 'True Parents', and he himself was generally known as 'Father' or 'Reverend Moon'. They were the ultimate authority in the Church, governing its practices and structures. And they lived in America, in New York State.

It was a more sober lecture than usual; Zack's lively style and sharp wit were not so much in evidence as they usually were. As he finished there was a moment's silence.

The discussion that followed was animated. The apathetic people were frankly incredulous. The 'neggers-out' produced arguments, of varying strength, to prove Zack wrong. Some asked careful questions, others wanted parts of the lecture repeated.

I sat quietly. I had nothing to say. There was too much to think about.

Amy looked at me curiously, obviously wanting me to confide in her. But I wasn't going to talk to Amy. She was too pushy. I wanted to go at my own pace.

When I saw Ruthie, the leader of my group, sitting apart from the others a little while later, I took the chance to talk to her. She was calm and approachable.

'How can I help you?'

'Well, I just wondered ...' I was hesitant, unsure of myself. Ruthie waited patiently. I started again:

'You know, hearing Zack's lecture tonight, and thinking about what Jessica and Zack have been teaching us all week – and then tonight, about Sun Myung Moon, being such an extraordinary person ...'

'You're right,' said Ruthie. 'He *is* an extraordinary person.' There was a note of awe, even reverence, in her voice.

'Well – do you think – because Zack said that the Lord of the Second Advent was going to be an Easterner, and he was born in the right year – do you think that Sun Myung Moon himself could possibly be the Messiah?'

There was a long pause. I'd said it. And yet, in saying it, I'd only given a focus to what had been bubbling in my mind for the past few days.

Ruthie answered slowly: 'I shouldn't say that to anybody else, Jacqui. There are people here who would find that sort of concept really difficult to understand yet.'

'Yes, but do you think that he is?'

'Well – it's possible, I agree. Yes, it's surely possible. It's a great thought, isn't it? But you see, Jacqui, I can't make up your mind for you. You must really pray about it, ask God to reveal his truth to you.'

Try as I might, I couldn't persuade Ruthie to say definitely what she thought of my suggestion, and I had no more success when I talked to the other leaders. The response was always the same: 'That's something you have to think through for yourself, Jacqui. You may well be right. We can't tell you.'

The consequence was that over the next few hours I began to be convinced in my own mind that Sun Myung Moon was a crucially important person in history – perhaps *the* most important person. I watched the others in the group, most of whom were leaving Camp K without realising this stupendous fact. I talked to few people that night. I hugged my new understanding to myself, comparing my situation to that of Mary in the New Testament: when she was told that the Messiah's approach was imminent, 'she pondered all these things in her heart'.

I had made a huge leap forward, I was sure. Cut loose from much that I had based my Christianity on before, I was desperate to make some kind of outward response to match my internal revelations. If they were indeed true, then it was perfectly possible that I, like the disciples 2,000 years ago, might one day see and even speak to the Messiah.

4 MUM

Some parents welcome their children's involvement [with the Unification Church], some tolerate it, some accept it with resignation, and some positively hate it.

[Constance Osmond, writing in *Parents: Magazine for Parents of Members of the Unification Church*, May 1980.]

With what seemed like a quiet inevitability, I was invited to stay on for a further week. There was no worry about money this time; I had handed over all that I had. I leaped at the chance to find out more, and the following Monday, as a new busload of visitors arrived, I took my place in the lecture room again and began to listen to the whole series again.

Now that I knew where the lectures were going, I picked up a great deal more than I had the first time round. The teaching of what I now knew as the Unification Church viewed history as a sequence of tragic failures. Adam and Eve were seduced by the serpent before they had reached the maturity that God had planned for them; ever since then, God's work has been aimed at undoing the evil of the fall and restoring mankind. But the history of mankind, the lecturers explained, is the history of man's failure to work with God in this process of restoration.

Cain, Satan's man, killed Abel, the man of God; Abraham failed to make the proper sacrifices; Moses struck the rock in anger; Solomon married ungodly women.

Divine Principle, on which the lectures were based, looked at the mission of Jesus in the same perspective – he was a perfect man who was betrayed by mankind. So although he achieved all that was in his power to achieve, his work came to an end with a crucifixion that God had never planned.

So who would God send to complete his work?

I knew the answer, but hearing it again thrilled me: *the Lord of the Second Advent*.

Carefully demonstrating his argument from biblical references, Zack – just as he had in the first week, though I had had so much to take in I hadn't absorbed it – described what the Lord of the Second Advent would be and do.

I took copious notes and after the lectures I read and reread them.

The second time round, I also had the opportunity to observe the leaders more closely. Some of them, I noticed, never ate breakfast, though they sat with us and joined in the conversation. I took every opportunity I could to talk with them, and to tell them the things I was beginning to believe about Sun Myung Moon.

Nobody put any pressure on me. In fact it was quite the opposite; only after I had talked several times to them did the leaders begin to tell me, gradually, over a period of days, that they themselves were followers of Sun Myung Moon.

Time was allowed in the daily schedule for private prayer. It wasn't a very long time, but I cherished every minute of it. I found myself talking to God in a new way, deeply conscious of the grief that he had felt at man's wickedness and the tragedy of Jesus's death on the cross. I had never thought of the cross in quite the same way before.

I thanked God constantly for bringing me to Camp K and opening up my mind. I saw myself as having been very definitely led to the group, and retraced events in my mind, conscious of God's guidance.

As I talked to the leaders and prayed on my own, meditating on the lectures and the conversations of the past fortnight, my entire view of God changed gradually and profoundly. I realised in a new and profound way that it was a suffering God whom I was contemplating, and that Jesus was a man who had suffered on a cosmic scale. Before, I had understood the suffering of the cross as a separation from God demanded by the fact that God was totally righteous and that, on the cross, Jesus was carrying all humanity's evil; but how much greater that suffering must have been, born of the knowledge that it might have been avoided, that the mission was a failure, that the plan of God had been thwarted!

When it was suggested that I should stay at the Camp a third week and hear the lectures yet again, I agreed immediately.

I was very tired by now. I had studied and talked virtually non-stop since my arrival. Also, during the second week, I had contracted blood poisoning in my leg as a result of an accident playing dodge-ball, and had hobbled painfully around Camp K for a day or two before the leaders asked what the problem was. When they saw my swollen and inflamed leg, they were appalled.

'You must see a doctor,' insisted Zack.

I grimaced. This was America. You couldn't just drop in to the local GP. Medical help had to be paid for, and most people had health insurance. As a visitor I hadn't bothered. It hadn't seemed worth it for a short stay. And I had no money of my own; no reply had arrived yet to the letter I'd written to my parents.

'Today, Jacqui,' urged Zack.

'I wish I could,' I said wryly. My leg was throbbing, and I was feeling a bit sick. Zack grasped the situation. 'Wait there, Jacqui,' he ordered, and left the room.

When he reappeared he was briskly efficient: 'Right,

Jacqui. This afternoon you're going to the medical centre to have that leg looked at.'

'But – the insurance!' I protested.

'That's all taken care of. You can be seen on mine.'

So I received medical attention and a supply of antibiotics. I didn't understand how the insurance was transferred, but Zack organised it for me. My leg responded well to the drugs, and soon I was feeling much better, despite my general tiredness. In any case, I was exhilarated by the fresh air, good food and mountain environment; and my brain was racing with scores of new ideas and perspectives.

A very strong element in the teaching at Camp K was the need for discipline in the Christian life, and the proper place of sacrifice and personal consecration. I discovered the reason for the leaders' absence at breakfast: they were fasting. Apparently it was a regular practice in the community among those who were deeply involved. I decided to go on a fast as well, for the whole of the third week. Nobody suggested it, or put pressure on me to do so. It was my own decision.

For seven days I ate nothing and drank only orange juice and milk. It wasn't too difficult; the calories in the drink took the edge off my hunger, and I was so absorbed in what I was doing that I hardly noticed the fact that I was not eating. The third week flew by.

I'd been in Camp K for three weeks, cut off from the outside world. Newspapers, television and radio had no place in the daily round of lectures, work and discussion. The world I'd left outside hardly impinged at all, there was so much going on.

Within this enclosed world I was beginning to find an identity. I knew I was one of the better students. I was keener to learn more, I knew more about the Bible to start with than many of the others; in discussion, I usually said the right things and often helped the leaders when the 'neggers-out' were particularly argumentative.

As I found my feet and began to talk more freely with the leaders about the way my thoughts were developing, they began to treat me as part of the community, and told me more about what life was like as a member of the Unification Church. 'We have experienced persecution,' I was told. 'Our parents have often turned against us, and there is so much misunderstanding. Many Brothers and Sisters have been really hurt …'

I'd had very little contact with my own family since arriving in the community. I had phoned once, and sent that brief letter telling them where I was, requesting funds. But that had been my only contact.

Which made it all the more astonishing when one day, at the end of the third week, my mother arrived at Camp K.

She was standing in the main drive beside a large car, oddly incongruous among the young people thronging the place. A man and a woman were with her, neither of whom I recognised.

'Mum!' I gasped. 'Whatever are you doing here? Oh' – I added hastily – 'it's great to see you.'

She opened her handbag and produced a single rose which she handed to me. 'I brought you this,' she said. Her voice was wobbly, as if she were on the verge of crying. I couldn't imagine why.

I took the rose and said thank you. It was rather crumpled; it hadn't survived the journey very well. There was an awkward silence. Mum introduced me to the couple. 'This is Mr and Mrs Winters. Mr Winters is the British Vice-Consul in San Francisco.' I shook hands warily. Mr Winters gave me a pleasant, neutral smile. 'They've been awfully kind,' Mum said. 'If they hadn't driven me out here it would have been a few days before I could get here.'

They were both tall and pleasant-looking. I discovered later that Mr Winters was on secondment from the Navy. I wasn't surprised – he had a military precision about his movements.

We went into a small chalet I'd not been in before. Mum looked around the room, at the Eastern furniture and the arrangements of fruit and flowers set out in Korean fashion on low tables. I thought it looked lovely, but it seemed to upset her. Her face was working, and she was trying to control herself. 'Mum – why *are* you here?' I suddenly felt panicky. 'There isn't anything wrong at home, is there?'

And then Mum lost control; she just broke down in tears. I hugged her, and felt her sobbing against me. 'Oh Jacqui – Why don't you come home? You must come home. Come home with me. You oughtn't to be here. You don't know what you've got yourself into. Don't you know what this place is all about?'

I tried to reassure her. 'Yes, Mum. I've just spent three weeks finding out. I want to stay here a while. Maybe a year! The college wouldn't mind.'

'But you don't understand—'

'It's OK, you needn't worry, honestly. I'm very happy here. Come on, why don't I show you round?'

We emerged into the sunshine. The Winters tactfully wandered off to sit in the car.

It wasn't the most relaxed guided tour that one could imagine, but I did my best and worked hard at being cheerful and painting the community in the best possible light. I desperately wanted Mum to be impressed.

As we returned, Mum pointed to the Winters's car. 'I want you to have a talk with Mr Winters,' said Mum. 'Please, Jacqui.'

'OK, Mum,' I agreed equably. I walked over to the car. Mr Winters leaned over and opened the door, and I sat down. Mrs Winters gave me a friendly smile.

'Look, Miss Williams,' her husband said a little awkwardly, 'I have to ask you some questions, just to make sure that you aren't going to get into trouble with the authorities here. Now, what papers do you have?'

I went to find my visa and work permit, and showed them to him. He grunted. 'These are in order,' he said.

'So what happens now? Are you going to have me thrown out of the country?'

'I couldn't even if I intended to,' he replied. 'Your papers are in good order. You've a right to be here.'

'Does that mean you're not working for my mother?'

He looked embarrassed. 'I'm not involved in all that, it's not my job.' He tapped my papers. 'But I may as well tell you, I've had a lot of trouble sorting out problems that people like you have got into with this particular group. Please, Miss Williams, do us all a favour – go home with your mother.'

I shook my head. 'I'm sorry, I can't do that. These people have got hold of something important, and I want to find out as much as I can about it. I'm staying here.'

'Be nice to her while she's here,' he said. 'She's come a long way.'

'I know that,' I retorted. We walked back to Mum in an uncomfortable silence. I hugged her. 'Come back tomorrow?'

'I thought it would be nice if you came to San Francisco for a few days,' Mum suggested hesitantly.

'I'm sorry,' I explained, 'I'd love to, but ...' Mum's face fell, and the Winters exchanged exasperated glances, not troubling to conceal their annoyance. 'We have such a strict timetable here ... It's the only way, you know? There's so much to be learned. Lots of people want to come. I'm really very lucky to be here at all.'

Mum came only once more. I was told as I left a lecture that she was waiting at the gate. I found her sitting at a table with an older white-haired woman. They looked tired and irritable, and I made a special effort to be welcoming.

'This is Norah Betts. I'm staying with her in San Francisco. She's been very kind.' I smiled at her. She looked frostily back.

We walked around Camp K, and Mum gave me family news, and I told her little stories of the things that had been happening to me, searching out the entertaining anecdotes and things that would put the community in a good light. Once or twice I managed to make her laugh.

Norah Betts hovered at our side. Her lips were set in a severe line. She didn't laugh at all. Her eyes darted here and there as if she were looking for something to make a fuss about. I was proud of the tidy paths and trim chalets, and the smiling Brothers and Sisters who were only too happy to be introduced to Mum.

Norah Betts maintained an icy silence until we found ourselves separated from Mum, who was some yards behind having a second look at a cabbage plot on which I'd been working that week. As we waited for her to catch up, Norah stared at me coldly.

'You've put your parents through all sorts of bother,' she said flatly. 'Thoughtless, selfish behaviour.'

Scarlet, I stammered, 'Whatever do you mean?'

'These people are deluded,' she retorted. 'Moon's a charlatan. How can you call yourself a Christian and get yourself mixed up in this sort of rubbish?'

'Now hold on a moment,' I said grimly.

'No, you just hold on a moment, young lady. Let me tell you a few facts about this Reverend Moon and his followers.'

She launched into a tirade of attacks on Sun Myung Moon, the community and the teachings of the Unification Church. Some of the things she said I recognised. The leaders had told me some of the charges that had been made against the movement, and it was obvious to me that they were unjustified. Other things that Norah Betts said I knew to be untrue from my own experience of four weeks in the community. But in any case, I wasn't going to listen. I was deeply offended, and it hurt to hear the people who had been so kind to me described in such a way.

Somehow I managed to stand back from the situation, and to be distant and objective as if I wasn't involved. *This is my first experience of persecution*, I told myself. *It was bound to happen sooner or later.* I listened to Norah Betts's tirade, and I could really see where she was coming from. In a strange way I even felt sorry for her.

'Look, Mrs Betts,' I said when she paused for breath. 'These people have given me hospitality, they have shared all sorts of things with me, we've read the Bible and prayed together, and I'm not going to call them charlatans. They have shown me real love.'

Mum was approaching, and Norah Betts fell silent.

It was a difficult and tense few hours, and I was dreading the time when we would say goodbye. As we embraced, Mum pleaded with me again. 'I can see that there are good things here, I really can. But Jacqui, we love you, we want you to be happy. Please come back to England with me.'

I squared my shoulders and looked her in the eyes, and said, 'Mum, I'm sorry, but I'm staying.'

It was the hardest thing I could remember ever having to say to her. We clutched each other, and again I could feel her sobs as she held me. Seeing her so frail and distraught, I felt almost as if I were the maternal one. But it was Norah Betts who led her gently away.

Mum stayed in San Francisco for a while after that, and she telephoned me several times. 'Will you at least come and see me in San Francisco?'

The leaders advised me strongly against it. 'We've had experience of Brothers and Sisters being kidnapped by their parents. It's better not to risk it. Which is more important –

to find out what God wants you to know, or to go and see your mother now?'

So though she telephoned three or four times, each time I said no. It was very hard, and Mum was extremely distraught, but I felt that God had given me this test, and the seven-day fast I'd taken had been a preparation.

But all the emotion was harrowing, because as a family we had never been particularly emotional. We never had arguments; Dad's word was accepted, even though sometimes grudgingly. This was my first outright attempt at total independence without their blessing.

Yet at the same time, I had an intense sense of direction and purpose. America was where I had to be. God had called me to California. It was because of that firm sense of assurance and purpose that I could stand my ground and refuse to be moved. Nothing anyone could do could change my mind. 'I'm sorry,' I said to Mum, 'and I know you're suffering because of what's happening, but this is where God wants me to be.'

I didn't want to alienate my mother; I loved her. But I felt that personal happiness was not the issue. What mattered was what God wanted. I wasn't callous. In my heart I was desperately sad. But I felt that I was given the courage and strength to go on.

So Mum went back to England without me, and I felt no guilt or remorse. I just felt very firm.

I didn't know until years later that Mr Winters had had to plead with the leaders at Camp K for my mother to be allowed to see me alone, nor that they had resisted the idea strongly. 'She's travelled 8,000 miles to see her daughter,' he had argued. 'You must allow her that. Nothing's going to happen. Please, let them talk.' They had finally relented.

I didn't know, either, that when Mum came that second time, she and Norah Betts had been kept waiting for two hours at the cantilever gate of Camp K, because nobody was prepared to call me out of the lecture. That was why they were so tired and tense when I appeared.

How much guilt or remorse I would have felt had I known that, I am not sure. Probably I would have been distressed but unmoved. God was dealing with me, I knew, and it would mean sacrifices and sadness. There was a cost to discipleship. Indeed, I would have been quite unmoved had I known that during her time in San Francisco, Mum had been talking a great deal with a Pulitzer Prize writer who knew Camp K and had researched the Unification Church thoroughly. The leaders had warned me about people like him. Satan used them to attack what God was doing through Reverend Moon.

But one fact of which I was completely unaware would have surprised me more than anything else could possibly have done. My mother did not tell me about it there and then partly because it was not something she wanted to talk about when there were so many other people around, and partly because she was herself so emotionally distraught that she did not trust herself to discuss it calmly.

The astonishing, incredible fact was that Mum, who had travelled half way across the world to appeal to me to come home, became a Christian in San Francisco, in the home of somebody she had met only days before.

The background to this astonishing news was that Norah Betts and her family, whose name had been given to Mum on the spur of the moment by the minister of my old church, had welcomed Mum into their home. They were a Christian couple, and Mum, who knew very few Christians in England, found their home an oasis of kindness in an anonymous city. While there, she found herself remembering some of the words of the Twenty-Third Psalm, and asked Norah for a Bible. That had been the beginning, and God, through the love and ministry of Mr and Mrs Betts, had made wonderful use of the five days which Mum had had to wait before she could visit me at Camp K.

She said nothing of it to me when she came to Camp K with Norah Betts. But it would not have deflected me from my new purpose. I doubt if it would even have made me rethink my own position. The very last thing I wanted was for God to take me away from California. I was now a follower of Sun Myung Moon, and I knew where I should be. All my thoughts were focused on this extraordinary person. I began to understand the reverence with which he was mentioned. In my heart, I was beginning to love him.

5   A BED OF ROSES

With the possible exception of the sale of ginseng tea,
which seems a consistent worldwide moneyraiser, there is
no single pattern of fund raising. It is different in each
country and for each stage of growth.

[Frederick Sontag, *Sun Myung Moon and the Unification
Church*, 1977.]

Annette knelt over the white polystyrene coffin-shaped
package and untied the strings. Carefully, she lifted the lid.
The roses inside, packed in ice, were arranged in neat rows.
Taking a single long-stemmed bloom, she handed it to me.

'It's lovely,' I said, admiring the morning light reflecting
off the drops of dew.

'Hold these,' said Annette, 'and I'll show you how to sort
them into bunches.'

Fascinated, I watched as she gave me my first lesson in
flower-selling.

Annette was one of the team leaders at the Bush Street house
in San Francisco, to which I had gone after leaving Camp K a
week or so earlier. It was a large building, and a large number
of people were staying there. I shared a room with three
other girls.

Leaving Camp K had been a strange experience. I would
very much have liked to have stayed on; not so much to hear
the lectures through a fourth time, but to stay with Jessica
and Ruthie and the other leaders. I had developed an

enormous respect and a great fondness for them over those few weeks. But besides that, I felt that I had matured in Camp K. I could only compare the situation to going on weekends away with other Christians when I'd been a teenager, and the desire one had to make the transition from somebody being led, to somebody who was leading. Then as now, it had been something I saw as a step in growing up as a Christian; and now, leaving Camp K, I felt that I was somehow different from the others who had gone through the workshop with me.

I'd gone there already a Christian; wanting to find out more about my faith. And I'd gone with expectations. I'd wanted – needed – to find companionship and love. On top of all that I genuinely believed that God had directed me to that place.

With all these extra dimensions to the workshop I felt I was different from the other people in my group. I felt I was a lot more aware of spiritual truth. It was easy for me, in the second and third weeks, to slip into the role of teacher, and reinforce the leaders as much as I could. Looking back from the vantage point of Bush Street, a normal house in a normal street with the gentle drone of traffic drifting in through the open windows, I confessed to myself ruefully that I had probably been unbearably smug and self-righteous up there on the hillside! But it didn't seem to matter anyway. *I was secure there*, I thought. *I contributed*.

'You see they have elastic bands round bottom and middle,' said Annette. 'That's no good, it strangles them. You have to take off the bands' – she slipped them off expertly – 'then you have to arrange them just so, with heads all one way. There.'

There was quite a system to it. The aim was to keep the roses as fresh as possible for as long as possible. They were long-stemmed budded tea varieties, very small and in different colours. They had to be repacked in lots of one

colour, with ice round their stems, and rewrapped in tissue.
A final outer wrapping of newspaper, and they were ready
for the street.

Flower-selling was one of the most wonderful things I had
ever done in my life, all the more so as I came to it after a few
days as a carpet cleaner.

In Unification Church terminology, one 'graduated' from
Camp K. I felt after my mother's visit that I had burned my
boats. Partly from necessity and partly from bravado, I now
considered myself a member of the community, and when it
was more or less assumed that I would be joining the
community at Bush Street, I willingly agreed.

The atmosphere was very different from what it had been
in the camp. There, however much I had felt a part of it all,
however much I had considered myself almost one of the
teachers, I had been a visitor, a student; somebody who
belonged to the outside. Back in San Francisco, in Bush
Street, by tacit agreement I had a very different status. I was
in the inner fold.

At Bush Street, for example, Sun Myung Moon was
referred to constantly, and given the title 'Reverend Moon',
or just 'Father'. He and his wife were known as 'True
Parents', and instead of hearing lectures about his writings, I
was able to read the writings themselves – usually copies of a
periodical publication called *Master Speaks*, which was a
transcript of his sermons.

There was a structure and a discipline to life in the house.
Everybody was under the leadership of an older member. To
my delight, Sam was also based at Bush Street, and he was
made responsible for me. I didn't find the discipline a
problem. Sam and I got on very well anyway. He often
called me one of his 'spiritual children' – a phrase, I
discovered, which Unification Church members often used
to describe those whom they personally had brought into
the movement.

Sam was the driver for a 'fundraising team'. Fundraising was one of several activities which were intended to raise money for the work of the movement. One of these was an office cleaning contract, which was how I came to be working as a carpet cleaner. But after only a few days, I was asked to join Sam's team.

Annette was joint leader of the team with Sam, and she looked after me for my first few days.

'I don't think I can do it,' I confessed to her, as we were loading the bundles of roses into the van. 'I never sold anything on the street before.'

Annette smiled placidly. 'You'll do fine,' she reassured me. 'Father has a good picture of how it is. When you sell a rose you're helping people to give to the Messiah. If a person buys one rose – just one single rose – it's as if an invisible thread reaches from their heart to the heart of the Messiah. I think that's beautiful.'

'Yes, that's really helpful,' I agreed, and it was a great help to me over the next few days when it took me most of a day to summon up the courage to approach a total stranger and ask him or her to buy a flower. If all that effort was making a difference in terms of the person's relationship with God – why, it was a tremendously worthwhile thing to be doing.

Soon I became much more at ease. Dropped in a strange street, I would make my way along, pushing my bunch of roses in front of passers-by.

'Hi, I'm Jacqui,' I accosted them. 'Would you like to buy a rose?'

Annette had passed on some tips for effective selling. The price was two dollars per rose, but we also sold them at two for three dollars. The 'one-for-two-but-two-for-three' approach worked amazingly well. People couldn't resist such a large discount. I became skilled at arranging the bunch in such a way that one or two slender blooms could be slid out without the rest of my careful display collapsing.

Flower-selling had its own jargon. I learned to watch out for 'bombers', buds that poked out from under the protective hood of newspaper into the warmth of the sun and began to open out. The name was an apt one, because they fell to pieces if you took them out.

For most of the day I jogged round the streets. The van drove me to one end of a street and dropped me, and then collected me at a designated pick-up point. The minute I climbed back into the van, Annette greeted me and took the roses from me; then I stretched out my legs and launched into a non-stop narrative of all that had happened in my area. It was all such an intense experience, and I had such a strong sense of mission in what I was doing, that the words just flowed out and I chattered away the whole time until the next dropping point. Annette was kind and attentive and heard me out sympathetically, occasionally asking a question or explaining some point or other.

The evenings were quite different. In the evenings we went bar-blitzing.

'Whatever's "bar-blitzing"?' I asked, when I first heard the expression.

'You get whole streets of bars here,' explained Sam, 'just bars and bars end to end, all sorts of different ones, like cowboy bars where they dress up in stetsons and listen to country music – all kinds of set-up. Bar-blitzing just means you start at one end – and blitz your way to the other.'

'What's it like?' I asked cautiously.

Annette shrugged her shoulders. 'It's quite scary,' she said. 'They're usually full of men, you don't see any women, not many. And some of them are real low dives.'

She was right, as I discovered when I began bar-blitzing.

The interior of the bar was very dark, and the walls seemed to be draped in black hangings of some kind. I stood at the door with Aggie – she had been with the community for several months and was an old hand at bar-blitzing.

'You work your way down that side,' whispered Aggie – rather incongruously in view of the music blaring within – 'and I'll go right down the far end and work my way back to you. We'll meet in the middle.'

'Whatever do I *do*?' I hissed back, watching the dim figures inside, some of the men dancing with the few women present, others standing in groups by the bar talking in loud, raucous voices.

'Sell flowers!' grinned Aggie, and plunged into the gloom. In the smoky haze at the end of the bar I saw her moving rapidly from person to person. I followed suit.

Taking my courage in both hands I marched up to the nearest man who looked at all approachable. He grinned warily as I advanced.

I only had one line of sales talk. I went straight into it. 'Hi! My name's Jacqui. Would you like to buy a rose?'

His neighbours guffawed, and he blushed. 'Uh-huh,' he muttered, shaking his head.

Greatly daring, I pushed harder. 'Buy one for your wife? Perhaps your girlfriend?'

'Yeah, Georgie – buy one for each of 'em,' spluttered a neighbour. He was looking at me in a rather unpleasant way. Georgie stood helpless. 'Ah – how much?' he said.

'One-for-two-dollars-two-for-three-dollars.' I rattled through my stock phrase smartly, then waited expectantly. Georgie considered for a moment, miserably. Then his face lit up. 'OK,' he capitulated, digging into his pocket. 'Here's three dollars, I'll take two.' As I delightedly slid my two nicest blooms from their wrapping for this, my first bar customer, he turned sheepishly to his friends. 'Gonna give 'em to my old lady,' he explained.

I took the three dollars and put the money in the carrier that I wore round my neck. *Thank you, Lord*, I said under my breath.

Then, out of a month's lectures, discussions and intensive reading, came a spontaneous and heartfelt further cry of gratitude. *And*, I added, *thank you, True Parents*.

I became quite expert at bar-blitzing. I learned to spot the people who would buy several roses, often just to get rid of me. I discovered that even people who could not be persuaded to buy flowers would often contribute small change if asked for a donation. And I learned to think and pray my way into good sales.

On the street I ran almost everywhere. If the street was nearly empty I carried a folded copy of *Master Speaks* in front of me and read it as I ran. While I ran I chanted. The others taught me several set chants – one very popular one was 'Glory to heaven and peace on earth: bless True Parents, success in their mission'.

Perhaps because I was running so much, perhaps because I was working long hours and getting much less sleep than I was accustomed to, I found myself on a permanent spiritual high. My energy and adrenaline kept up with my emotional excitement. We were encouraged to set ourselves goals. At first my goals were very small. If I set myself a goal of fifty dollars to be collected that day, for example, I chanted 'Five-zero, five-zero', until I made my first sale, say of two dollars. Then I chanted 'Forty-eight to go, forty-eight to go,' and so on until I had reached my goal.

For the first time in my life I had a sense of real spiritual power. People bought flowers, often the most unlikely ones; perhaps they were amused at the sight of the tall English girl running down the sidewalk, chanting rhythmically and clutching a much-folded magazine in her hand. Whatever the reason, prayer and chanting worked; we gained entrance to some extraordinary places, and we sold a great many roses.

Going into bars, with their choking atmosphere and dark shadows, I sometimes felt that power again. I knew that I was invading a world of evil and secrecy and hopelessness, carrying in my arms the means by which each soul in that place could be linked with the heart of God. It made selling roses not only a privilege but a power. Many of my customers bought them from me not because they wanted the flowers, nor because they wanted to support our work; they bought because I had come in from outside, from the sunlit sidewalk and the open highway, and they were in a world of shadows.

Much of the teaching I received in the first few days centred on that concept of energy and life. 'You have to push out negativity,' Sam explained. 'Cain killed his brother, and paid the price. We all have Abel-sides to ourselves and also Cain-sides. We have to conquer the Cain-side, the negative side.'

I nodded; it made sense. I'd been taught about Original Sin years before, when I first began finding my way round the Bible; Sam's explanation took it a stage further, into the realm of my daily living. The things I did wrong were tied in to the historic fall of the human race. Yes, I was Abel's daughter and Cain's daughter. It fitted. I determined to cultivate the Abel in me. I wasn't going to Cain-out, not if I could help it.

'So when you chant, when you set yourself a goal, you're pushing out negativity,' added Sam. 'You're directing your concentration; that way you overcome your weaker side.'

In truth, failure would have been impossible to deal with at that stage of my new life. I was revelling in a 'honeymoon' experience, and was incapable of coming to terms with anything less than absolute success. My companions and leaders buoyed me up constantly; any amount, however small, that I made selling roses was praised, and the experience of exceeding a previous day's sales by even five dollars was greeted as a superb achievement.

Part of me realised this and was grateful for it; I was

sensible enough to recognise that I was being given a very gentle introduction to life in the community, and that almost everybody was working much harder than I was.

But another part of me was aware, right from the beginning, that I was actually rather good at street selling. I found that I could spot likely customers and close the sale quickly. It took me almost no time at all to know when I was talking to somebody who was never going to buy, however aggressively or charmingly I talked; so I spent more time selling and wasted less time on no-hopers. As a beginner, I worked fewer hours than many of the others; I came back with less money; but I was making much more per hour, and making much better use of my time on the street.

'Success' in this situation did not mean commercial success. As I tipped my bag of money out to be counted after working an area, I hardly ever viewed it as wealth either for myself or for the community; I had been taught not to. We never viewed the money as cold cash. For the people we had persuaded to buy from us, it was a lifeline towards salvation, a means of grace.

And it seemed I had some sort of gift for this work. I did not discount all the praise I was receiving as mere kindness to a beginner. I could see that I was doing well, that I was of some use to the group. That fact, together with the very positive experiences I was having in the community and on the street, fed my growing feeling that things were going right. Any doubts which momentarily troubled me, when I compared my new lifestyle with the kind of orthodox evangelical church life I would by then have been involved in had I gone home as planned, were easily laid to rest when I considered the many ways on which God seemed to be blessing my new life.

Half a world away, in my old orthodox evangelical church in Windsor, my mother was now a member of the fellowship. Church had never been of any particular importance in her life before, but now everything had changed. Out of her abortive trip to San Francisco, in the most unlikely circumstances possible, God had chosen to do something miraculous in her life.

And at that same church, the members began to meet every Saturday morning to pray for me, pleading with God that I would be delivered from the teaching of Sun Myung Moon.

6 RELATIONSHIPS

By having children, Adam and Eve would have become the God-centred True Father and Mother – the True Parents of mankind. If Adam and Eve had formed this first God-centred family, then out of that would have come a God-centred tribe, a God-centred nation, and a God-centred world in which God alone would be the ruler. Then perfection would have reigned from the beginning to eternity.

[Sun Myung Moon, *The New Future of Christianity*, 1974.]

Our team that lived in the house on Bush Street was a small one. There were the leaders, Sam and Annette, of whom I had grown very fond. Two older people, Fred and Kristy, lived in the house and came out with us in the van occasionally. Joseph, Hugh and Aggie were like me, Brothers and Sisters who had only recently joined and were new to the community.

We were not the only people in the house – in fact it was quite crowded. Other teams lived there, and also people who worked locally and came in for lectures, meals and discussions. Not everybody worked on Unification Church projects like the food warehouse, and not everybody actually lived in the house.

Though in many ways the house and my new lifestyle were just as I had hoped for when I was trying to find a Christian community to join, other things weren't quite as I had expected. For example, I saw very little of Joseph, Hugh and Aggie except for the time we were together in the van travelling between streets or when I was working with one of them bar-blitzing. In the evenings I was too tired to talk much, and what talking I did was usually with Sam and Annette or a visitor.

I loved meeting new people. Every night we all ate together, and there were usually strangers present who'd been invited to come just as I had been invited by Sam back in the San Francisco bus station. There would be songs and other entertainment from members of the community – I sometimes played a guitar or sang – and then after the meal we would sit and talk with the visitors.

Talking was one of the great things about the Bush Street house. You only had to be sitting next to somebody for that person to strike up a conversation and show a genuine interest in you. It was talk without gossip. There was no backbiting. I found myself comparing it with the kind of conversations there had been at the camp in Cheboygan, half a continent away and belonging to a summer that seemed to have happened years ago.

People were not inquisitive; I wasn't cross-examined about my past. Indeed I rarely said much about my life in England. Conversation tended to be about experiences I'd had fundraising, or other things I'd been doing that day.

Even preparing the food was satisfying. We all took our turn, and also helped with cleaning and other household chores. We set to these jobs with great energy and enthusiasm, and we talked about them as work done for God, in just the same way that we talked about our work on the streets, selling roses to raise funds.

And behind everything was the teaching, whether in formal lectures, *Master Speaks*, books such as *Divine Principle*, or discussions and conversations that often went on late into the night. The lectures and seminars of Boonville and Camp K were reinforced by constant restating and expanding in the daily life of the community. If anybody had told me, six months before, that I would be part of a group that carried round with it volumes of the teaching of a religious leader from the East who claimed to be bringing a message that went beyond the Bible, I would have dismissed the notion as being a fantasy about a totalitarian system of a kind which I would never join.

But it didn't seem like that. How can one force food on a hungry person? You can only coerce somebody *against* his or her will. And I wanted to know more. I was desperate to find out as much as I could.

Neither did it seem like a dry, intellectual system that I was being taught. We prayed, alone and in groups, and the praying was part of the teaching. My own praying changed. Like the rest, I began to pray to 'True Parents', where I had always prayed in the name of Jesus. The change was undramatic. I fell into the new way of praying partly because that was how everybody else in the community prayed, and it was a little like picking up the 'jargon' of a new group. But also, the teaching I had received – particularly the three weeks of lectures at Camp K – had prepared me for accepting that Reverend Moon was the Lord of the Second Advent. For me, he was Jesus in another human form.

I'd never thought a great deal about the Godhead, and certainly hadn't compartmentalised God into three boxes. I knew that God the Father had a particular role, that Jesus's work revolved around the cross, and that the Holy Spirit had been sent as a comforter and to be the presence of God in the world. But in terms of the persons of God, I saw everything as centring on Jesus. And all the emotional and spiritual relationship I'd felt for him I simply transferred to Reverend Moon, for I had decided that he *was* Jesus. The transfer was made easier because in the Church we were constantly told that we should love True Parents with all our hearts and minds.

I had no clear picture in my mind of Mrs Moon, but I found it easy to pray in the name of True Parents. Apart from anything else, it reflected the joy and intimacy of the relationships I was finding in that community; prayer flowed out of life.

Relationships, I soon discovered, were at the heart of the Unification Church's teachings.

Very early on I realised that there were no couples among the people at Bush Street. There were not many married people. Moses Durst was married, I knew, even though his wife hadn't been there when I heard him lecture that first night. But not only were there few married couples, nobody seemed to be engaged or even courting. I found this strange by comparison with other Christian groups I had known, where, because everybody was sharing a common concern and had similar interests, there would usually be at least one or two couples who were either going out together or engaged.

Because it was such a new environment to me, I saw nothing at all sinister in this, but it did strike me as unusual. One day I was washing dishes with Kristy, and managed to manoeuvre the conversation around to the topic. We had been talking about a church I'd attended in England.

'They were good people,' I explained to her. 'But there were problems.'

Kristy, who was a large, comfortable person, selected a dripping plate and carefully dried it. 'What sort of problems?'

'Well – relationships, mainly. You know, you weren't expected to have any deep friendships with men who weren't Christians ...'

'That seems fair enough,' commented Kristy.

I conceded the point. 'But they went further than that – they seemed to rule out friendships outside the church, even.'

Kristy thought for a moment before answering, moving the rough dishcloth in slow, deliberate circles around an earthenware plate. 'But if,' she volunteered, 'your church really knew what was best for you – knew better than anybody, even you yourself did – then wouldn't it be much the best thing to let them make that kind of judgment?'

'Well of *course* it would,' I replied. 'But they didn't know, did they?'

'Sounds like they didn't, I guess.'

I reached for the next stack of plates and slid them, one by one, into the hot water. There was a companionable silence, interrupted for a while only by the slapping of dishwater and the clink of crockery.

'What happens here?' I asked.

'How do you mean?'

'Well, what does the Unification Church teach about relationships like that? I mean, do people here only go out with people from the community?'

Kristy considered. 'You're asking a big question, you know. I guess that touches on just about everything that goes on here. You really have to get to grips with what marriage is all about.'

'So what *is* it all about?'

'It's to do with perfect family. You know what *Divine Principle* says. When Adam and Eve fell, they spoiled God's plan for them to set up a perfect family. When Jesus died on the cross it meant that *he* couldn't set up a perfect family. He was let down by humanity. So God is still wanting perfect family. Right?'

I nodded. These were teachings that I now knew by heart. I'd even taught them to others.

'Well then; it was Eve talking to Adam that caused their problems. While she was talking to him she was deceiving him, distracting him from God. Father says she was multiplying evil. Now, you think about what it's like when two people start to fall in love with each other. A lot of nothings get said. You know that.'

'OK ...' I said doubtfully. I'd always thought the idle chatter of courting couples to be pretty harmless.

'In this community, we discourage casual relationships. It's all too important for that. You won't see anybody dating here. In fact it's forbidden.'

I stacked the last plates and unplugged the sink. The water swirled noisily down the waste pipe. 'Forbidden?' I echoed.

'If you find that you're beginning to feel more than a brother-sister friendship – if you think you might be falling in love – then you should report it to one of the leaders.'

'What happens then?'

Kristy inspected a plate critically before wiping it briskly. 'Then you get moved, you move on to another part of the family in another city. Maybe in another State. That way' – a final vigorous wipe of the dishcloth – 'temptation's taken out of your way.'

A picture of Sam – tall, relaxed, brown and healthy from his long hours working out-of-doors – flashed across my mind. Was Kristy hinting at something? I stole a quick glance at her. She was busily wringing out the dishcloths and hanging them over the hot water pipes to dry. Her face betrayed nothing.

I went back in my mind over the times I'd spent with Sam. I'd felt completely relaxed with him from the start. I remembered the ease with which I'd talked to him, and the complete understanding he'd demonstrated. I thought of the long hours of discussions at Camp K, and the disappointment when he'd left and Amy had taken his place as my guide and advisor; then of my delight when I'd returned to the house in Bush Street and found that he was there.

Was I becoming too fond of Sam? The thought threw me into confusion; not just because I was facing up to the disturbing thought that I might have entered into a relationship I hadn't thought through (and of which Sam might not even be aware, let alone appreciate …), but also because I was suddenly alarmed by the possibility that the leaders of the community might think that I was falling in love with Sam and send me far away. And whatever I felt about Sam, I was certainly becoming very attached to the community at Bush Street.

I didn't pursue the matter with Kristy, but left it hanging. Afterwards, I thought and prayed about it for a long time. Eventually I decided that I wasn't in love with Sam, that it truly was a sister-brother friendship that we had, and Sam said nothing to make me feel otherwise. After a day or two I stopped interpreting every casual glance as a token of love, and went back to the easy-going, affectionate relationship I'd had with him before my conversation with Kristy.

Some questions were still unanswered, however, and I waited for the opportunity to find out more. Not long afterwards I found myself again working with Kristy and took up the topic again.

We were preparing a meal with some other people in the kitchen, and found ourselves sitting side by side, apart from the rest, peeling potatoes. I broached the subject again.

'Kristy,' I said tentatively, 'we were talking the other day; you know, about relationships.'

'Uh-huh,' said Kristy.

'I understand what you said about friendships and how that can be a problem, and how all that fits in with *Divine Principle*. But something's still bothering me.'

'What's that?'

'Well – if people are discouraged from dating each other, and I can see why that's necessary, it makes sense – but how do people get to know each other well enough to get married?'

Kristy waited a while before answering. 'The aim of creation was to set up a perfect family. The restoration of creation is going to be the uniting of man and woman, in relationship with each other and with God, raising perfect children and taking dominion over all things. That's what Father says.'

She was paring a potato, over and over, long spirals curling into the bucket beneath. She continued, picking her words slowly.

'We are working towards establishing a new generation. We're beginning to put into practice those things. So it's much too important to be left to factors like who you fancy, or who you feel attracted to. Don't you think?'

'I see,' I agreed. It made sense. Everything that the community taught seemed to make sense. It was all very logical. That was one of the things I liked about it.

'So what *is* important,' Kristy went on, 'is who is best for you in terms of that new world that's coming. And we don't talk very much about it, because when the time is right you'll know. Father will know. Then there is the Blessing, when Father matches couples. Like being engaged, but much more special.'

'But how does he know which Brothers and Sisters are suited for each other?'

Kristy looked surprised. 'Oh, that's no problem,' she said matter-of-factly. 'He knows. Father knows.'

Kristy made it plain that she didn't want to discuss the matter at any length, and I found that the leaders and the older members were all similarly reticent about 'matchings' and 'blessed couples'. It wasn't exactly a grand conspiracy of silence; it was just that the subject was never voluntarily broached by them, and if somebody tried to provoke a conversation on those topics, the bare minimum was said and the subject changed.

After a while I lost interest in the matter. I wasn't thinking about marriage anyway, and I was much too busy for any relationship like the boyfriends I'd had in England.

But it remained a romantic ideal, a hope for the future. I

was satisfied with my relationship with God and was thrilled at the new discoveries I was making about him and his plans for my life. Yet in another sense I was conscious of a yawning emptiness in my life, emphasised by a sense of aloneness which my aloofness from the other new members only served to highlight. I hoped that there would be somebody for me in the future.

In the meantime, I threw myself into fundraising, working in the house, and learning as much as I could.

7 HOUSTON

Houston: City (1978 est. pop. 1,460,000), SE Texas, a deepwater port on the Houston Ship Canal ... Houston is a port of entry, a great industrial, commercial, and financial hub, one of the world's major oil centres, and the third-busiest tonnage-handling port in the United States.

[*The International Geographic Encyclopaedia and Atlas*, Macmillan Press, 1979.]

'We're putting a new fundraising team together, Jacqui,' announced Jessica, 'and you'll be joining it.'

I was delighted. I had been at the house in Bush Street for over three weeks, but I was still only fundraising part-time; the rest of the week I was working in the house or learning more about the Unification Church. Sometimes I became quite restless as I watched the van leave in the morning, wishing I could go with those who would be out fundraising that day. While they were gone the house was nearly empty, and it was hours before everybody came back, exhausted and full of stories of the day's events.

'That's great!' I exclaimed. 'Who'll be leader? Who else will be on it? When do we start?'

Jessica smiled. 'You're keen! That's good. Joshua has the details.'

Joshua was Jessica's brother-in-law. Together, they ran the San Francisco operation. He was a calm, relaxed person.

'Well, there'll be six Brothers and Sisters in all.' He ran

through the names. I didn't know any of the others particularly well. 'And Sam will be leader.'

I beamed; Sam was by now a close friend, and he was my 'spiritual father'. I was used to going to him for help and advice; he'd explained so many things to me and it was through him that I was in the Unification Church anyway. I was delighted that I was going to be on his team.

'OK?' smiled Joshua. 'Right – you leave for Houston tomorrow morning.'

'Houston?' I stammered.

'Sure – that's where the team will be based. Didn't you know?'

'Uh – no, Jessica didn't say.'

Joshua was reassuring. 'Well, don't worry. You'll enjoy it. There's a home church there, witnessing. The Mobile Fundraising Teams have worked there. But you'll be part of a resident fundraising team. The money you raise will help fund the work here.' He looked me squarely in the eyes, with a serious expression: 'We think you'll do well, Jacqui. Don't let Father down. You're part of his mission.'

My first reaction was one of fear. I didn't want to leave. I was accepted in San Francisco. I was getting to know people and I was becoming familiar with the work. I was learning, too; every day I studied *Divine Principle*. Couldn't I stay in San Francisco and join a team there full time?

In the few hours before I was due to leave, I talked things over with Kristy.

'I'm a bit worried,' I confessed.

As I had known she would, Kristy encouraged me to go. That was why I had talked to her. 'Why in particular nervous?' she asked.

'I don't think I'm ready yet. I'm the youngest on the team.'

'And when d'you think you *would* be ready?'

I laughed. 'Yes, I see what you mean ... maybe it's good that the decision was made for me.'

Kristy nodded. 'You'll find that decisions like that usually are made for you in the Family,' she said. 'It's part of our service to one another and to the world outside. And when you've been in Houston a while, you'll know it was the right time to go.'

'We'll fundraise all the way out,' said Sam, spreading the map out smooth on the bumpy grass.

It was the next day, and we were sitting on the roadside fifty miles out of San Francisco, having lunch. It was hot, and the interior of the van was sweltering. It was good to be in the open air again.

'We'll be heading *this* way,' Sam indicated the highway out of California into Nevada. 'We'll work the gambling joints, the bars, the night spots – anywhere people gamble and have loose money. *Here*' – he indicated the Lake Taho area – 'there are lots of casinos, plenty of big rollers. Then there's Vegas, Phoenix – all good places. We have to make this trip last, we'll check out the small places on the way.'

It was a big challenge because it was all virgin territory for the Unification Church. And it was important that once we got to Houston we should fundraise systematically.

I remembered Joshua's parting words as we'd left early that morning: 'The worst thing that can happen to a fundraiser is to find himself in an area somebody did last week. People often think of us as a one-off. You get people saying "Oh, right, I gave to you people already, you got my money last week." So you have to make sure you do the job right first time. You might find that people have cooled off if you go back.'

It took us three weeks to get to Houston. We travelled at night, and one of us always sat with Sam to make sure he didn't fall asleep; the rest of us slept on top of the polystyrene boxes of roses that were piled in the back of the van.

In those three weeks American towns flashed by, like an atlas looked at briefly and only half-remembered. Places blurred together in my mind: Phoenix, San Diego, Santa Hanna, Lake Tahoe, Dallas, Odessa, Midland, Fort Worth, Austin ... the catalogue of towns and cities that we passed through was a long one, and included several that I had wanted to visit. But all I saw of them was endless bars, shops and gambling venues – anywhere where there were people with money. We ate in hamburger bars that all looked the same, and at night we told one another how we'd done and then fell asleep.

As we came down through Texas into Austin and then Houston we found ourselves in oil country. 'Loads of money here!' grinned Sam, as we had our first sight of the massive refineries and oil pipelines. Everywhere we went we saw construction work in progress.

Houston itself was big, hot and flashy, with enormous commercial buildings and all the trappings of a prosperous modern city. In our first few days we rented a bungalow, and made arrangements to collect our stock of roses from the airport as and when we needed new supplies. They were bought from a huge supplier in Texas, and arrived packed in ice as they had in San Francisco.

Like many things in the bungalow, the roses were a link with the life I'd left behind after such a short time in San Francisco. Just as we had there, we spent hours each week preparing the stock, picking out the fragile ones and the wilting ones, freshening them up by picking off the damaged outside petals, and making sure that they were sold before they wilted again – as they surely would – and fell to pieces. We tried as hard as we could to make the flowers look nice, because it was so demoralising to have to try to sell flowers that looked horrible.

Annette's training stood me in good stead.

But there were many other things that were different, and some I found disturbing.

It was the first time, for example, that I had come across

systematically working through a city, dividing it into areas and methodically fundraising in industrial premises, shops and the night spots. Sam was a good organiser. In the daytime we worked through the industrial locations and the shops; at night we went door-to-door in residential areas, when people were home from work, and then went on to the bars and the nightclubs.

The night life of Houston was a shock, and an unpleasant one. There were bars of all descriptions; in a Hell's Angel bar, for example, inhabited by black-leathered, long-haired men and hard, larger-than-life women, I panicked and tried to leave. The music was from a heavy metal band, and I really felt that it was inciting an atmosphere of hatred and malevolence that was in some way directed at me. People were staring at me and muttering unpleasantly to one another.

Every time before, when fundraising, I'd felt in control of the situation. I had my flowers and my sales patter, and I reckoned I could handle any situation. But this was different. I wasn't in control, and I had over two hundred dollars in my bag.

A six-foot Angel lurched up to me, looked me full in the face, and pulled a rose from my bunch. 'What's this?' he said softly.

'I'm selling them,' I said faintly. 'Would you like one? Two dollars, or you can have two for three dollars.'

The familiar ritual had no effect. He held the rose up at arm's length, as if daring me to reach up for it. I remained motionless. His lip curled. He let go of the rose. It fell to the floor. Still holding my gaze, he reached out his foot and deliberately crushed the flower.

His friends applauded wildly. He turned away. Suddenly hands were reaching towards me from all sides, plucking handfuls of roses from the bunch. I clutched what was left and tried to push my way towards the door. *Help me, God,* I prayed, *please help me* ... Miraculously, the crowd parted to let me through. I emerged shaking and in tears, feeling almost as if it were myself rather than my product that had been violated.

There were many scary situations and many bad experiences. We sold product in gambling dens, in gay bars and nightclubs which were obviously being used as fronts for prostitution. But we persevered.

Hardest of all to cope with were the sex shops and strip clubs.

'I can't go in *there*,' I protested, when I was given my first assignment in that part of town.

Sam rebuked me. 'Do you think the people in there don't deserve to hear the truth, and have the chance to find God?'

I blushed scarlet. 'Of course I don't ... But I couldn't go inside, it would be dangerous – perhaps one of the men? ...'

Sam shook his head. 'I could ask Rick or Mal to go, but that's not how it is. They have their own part of the mission. Yours is to work these shops today. That's your area. You'll be with Louise.'

Louise had been in the Church for over a year, and was confident and at ease with strangers. But she was as apprehensive as I was.

We went into our first shop together. It was a grubby shopfront, boarded over, painted black; inside, it was a few moments before our eyes adjusted to the electric light. It looked fairly ordinary; racks of magazines leaned against the walls, there were some posters which I looked at once and then averted my eyes from, and there were shelves and cabinets displaying what looked like black frilly nightgowns and leather harnesses. A young man in jeans, his shirt open to the waist, was sitting at the counter reading a magazine with his feet up; on a hidden loudspeaker, barely audible music tinkled and lurched in the background. An oppressive odour of stale tobacco smoke and oriental incense lingered in the room.

We took in very little of it; as we came in, several men browsing in the magazines glared at us in a mixture of annoyance and furtiveness, and the young man at the counter uncoiled his legs and stood up.

'What do you want?' He appeared slightly amused.

We spoke in near-perfect unison: 'Do-you-want-to-buy-a-flower?'

He might have agreed, but we didn't wait to find out. Our prepared speech delivered, our nerves failed completely and we took to our heels. We plunged back into the daylight and ran as fast as we could for two blocks. Then we came to an incoherent stop.

'Did you *ever*!' gasped Louise.

I drew in my breath in rasping gulps. 'All those magazines! Did you see the covers? And those awful men ...'

Louise and I looked at each other, and then we began to laugh. Our laughter was slightly hysterical.

Finally we sobered up. 'What do we do now?' I demanded.

Louise set her shoulders and thrust a determined chin forward. 'We go right back,' she said.

I took some convincing, but she was quite right. 'If what we're doing is of any importance at all, what are we doing running away?' she pointed out.

So we plucked up our courage and went back, and, amazingly, we actually sold some flowers.

We always hated going into the sex shops and the clubs. There was always an atmosphere of real evil in them. I suppose that if I had been asked beforehand what sort of person ran them, I would have said perverted old men; but in fact they were usually young people, some as young as I was. We soon realised that there were some very nasty people indeed involved, and that some of the premises were merely fronts for drug rackets and other criminal activities. And though we could only steel ourselves for the briefest glimpses at the magazines and books in the shops, we could see that it was very hard pornography that was on offer. We knew that we were running serious risks just by hanging around such places.

But we were driven by a compulsion. We had to give people the opportunity to buy from us. That thread from the heart of the Messiah had to be extended to everybody, even if at the end of the day we were thrown out on the streets and customers were left with a handful of wilting roses.

And one day, the risks flared up into a really frightening incident.

It was like a scene from a nightmare, from a bad B-film. A man was striding after me, conspicuous in a tartan jacket. He was keeping a few yards behind, easily matching my own half-running, half-stumbling pace. I snatched another look behind; he was staring determinedly at me, pushing aside people on the sidewalk who got in his way. I'd hoped to lose myself in the crowds. It wasn't working. I wasn't going to get away.

It had been quite a classy little bar, one of two or three in a side street, the sort you aren't allowed to enter if you're wearing jeans. A bored-looking singer lounged on a rostrum and crooned into a microphone; a pianist improvised listlessly at the keyboard. I stood at the front door, clutching my armful of roses, and looked helplessly at the smartly dressed, supercilious people thronging the bar. I knew it wasn't going to be my night.

I'd adopted my usual strategy; to go through to the far end and work my way out again, selling roses as I went. I put on my brightest smile and rehearsed my sales pitch. 'Hi! I'm Jacqui. I'm selling flowers. We're collecting for work with kids, we help drug addicts, take them in off the streets, would you like one rose for two dollars or maybe two for three dollars?'

At first I'd had high hopes of the man in the tartan jacket. He asked lots of questions, and examined the roses carefully, as if he were choosing which he was going to buy. But then his questions turned to me, who I was, what I was doing in Houston; I noticed that he had very bright eyes, and that he was watching me as I talked, with a very strange expression indeed. I became wary.

'So how many roses would you like?' I'd demanded abruptly. He grinned slowly. 'Hold hard, Miss—Jacqui, that right? Well, Jacqui, a purchase like this, lotta dough, sure needs careful thought.'

Was he serious, or just fooling around? Perhaps this was going to be a really great sale – and I'd had a really bad bar run so far that evening. I decided to string along, and smiled wanly. 'Fine! I'll be around.'

I'd moved away and approached other people, but had no luck at all. They either ignored me completely or turned away with withering comments. At last I was nearing the exit. Giving up my hopes of sales, I grabbed everything and made for the door. Out of the corner of my eye I'd seen the tartan man following. I could tell by the look on his face that he wasn't interested in roses at all. It was me he was interested in.

I'd hoped he'd give up when I left the bar, but now he was pursuing me in the open street. I considered shouting for help, but decided against it. He looked a bit mad. He could turn violent for all I knew. I just wanted to be rid of him.

On the far side of a small parking lot a dark, cavernous door was marked with a trim sign. It was another bar.

I thought very fast. If I went in and he followed me, I would be trapped. On the other hand, there would be people in there, potential witnesses. Surely he wouldn't try anything?

The man was coming closer. Making a snap decision, I plunged into the gloom, and found myself in a cool, panelled lounge, lit by a few weak electric lamps. The man appeared in the doorway behind me and advanced cautiously into the gloom. A handful of people were sitting at tables. I pushed past them to the bar itself. A heavily made-up woman and two men were arguing. They ignored me. I headed for the safety of the toilet cubicles at the far end of the room.

Slamming the cubicle door shut, I slid the bolt. Trembling, gulping huge gasps of air partly from breathlessness and partly from fear, I waited for the sound of footsteps approaching my refuge. None came. All I could hear was the insistent hammering of my heart and the voices of the trio at the bar rising stridently.

As my pulse rate subsided, I became intrigued. Laying my flowers carefully on the toilet seat, I pressed closer to the door, trying to make out what the argument was about.

It seemed that one of the men was the woman's husband, the other her lover. Accusations and counter-accusations flew to and fro. I stealthily slid the bolt back and opened the door a crack. The woman was behind the bar. She looked middle-aged, her hair piled inexpertly in a large blonde beehive on top of her head; the two men looked like truck drivers, heavy drinkers.

Suddenly a gunshot exploded above the uproar.

For a split second there was an absolute, shocked silence. Then everybody began shouting simultaneously. I held the door almost closed and peered cautiously across the room; a flash of tartan was disappearing through the door. At least one problem was solved.

'Get the cops!' shouted a frightened voice. I jerked into action. I didn't want to hang around to be questioned by the police. My heart pounding again, I grabbed my flowers, pushed the door open and emerged into the main lounge.

A crowd of people was gathered round the bar. The woman was screaming, a high-pitched sobbing wail that went on and on. Everybody was pushing towards the bar, fighting for a glimpse of the bulky shape lying on the floor. Only one of the two men was visible, held by two or three others against the wall. On the bar itself, a stubby revolver lay in full view.

I realised that the shape was the body of one of the men. It wasn't moving. As my fear turned to incredulity, and I absorbed the fact that I had just missed seeing a murder, chaos broke out in the bar as people began running all over the place and arguing at the tops of their voices.

Tears were pouring down my cheeks, though they were a reaction of shock rather than of grief for the man who lay dead; I could barely take in the fact that it had happened. Numbly, I picked my way through the crowd and burst through the doorway into the bright parking lot outside. In the distance the rise and fall of the first police sirens droned through the streets.

I knew the neighbourhood streets slightly. We'd worked them only a day or two previously. It was a network of parallel blocks. I doubled back and forward until I came to a street I recognised. I was only a few hundred yards from the pick-up point, where the van would be waiting.

As I turned the last corner I saw the vehicle waiting. The familiar Chevrolet with its blue and yellow Californian registration plate, parked awkwardly in a small lay-by, looked like a haven of beauty and peace at that moment. As I grabbed the door handle and tumbled in, I was still clutching my flowers.

Inside, surrounded by my friends, I broke down and sobbed hysterically for several minutes before I was able to tell them what had happened. Afterwards, we prayed together, and I was allowed to take things easy for the rest of the afternoon.

Half an hour later, alone in the van with Sam and Louise, I went over what had happened again. Just telling it made it more manageable.

When I'd finished, Louise was silent for a while. Then she grinned. 'At least you kept hold of the flowers,' she said comfortably. 'You saved the product. That's good. Can't have been easy.'

I looked at the bundle of rose blooms, crumpled in their paper sheath. 'I'm afraid they're a bit the worse for wear.'

'They'll freshen up,' said Louise, and picked up a handful of the blooms. Carefully, she stroked the petals closed and skilfully plucked the most battered leaves from the stalks. 'Yes, they'll do fine,' she pronounced. 'Worth two dollars of anybody's money.'

I began to feel better.

Such incidents made me very aggressive. I learned to speak to people in a raised voice, willing them to buy. We discovered the significance of 'eye-contact', and the fact that very few people can handle being looked straight in the eyes. I used it to good effect to intimidate shy people, or to win over the aggressive ones. I think that the ability to confront people and not show real fear is one reason why I wasn't raped or attacked.

My determination, in a difficult situation, was always to get out, alive, with my flowers intact. I was much more angry if anybody threatened my flowers than if I was personally threatened. My whole way of life was now intimately bound up with those roses, and I identified with them totally.

It was much more than a nine-to-five job. We were out all hours of the day. Work was the whole of our life. We had a tremendous sense of responsibility; we were never casual about it. Our experiences were all intense, whatever we were doing. *Everything* was important.

When letters from home arrived it was like receiving news from a distant planet. People and situations which had involved me deeply before I left home in early summer now seemed irrelevant. Church leaders, friends and wise counsellors from the past all became shadowy, half-remembered figures as the excitement of being in the front line for God gripped me.

A letter arrived from somebody in England whom I had once regarded as my spiritual mother. Linda and her husband had been very helpful to me when I was searching to know more about the work of the Holy Spirit; they had prayed with me and laid hands on me, and my Christian life had taken a large leap forward.

That had been a long time ago, when I was seventeen, before I went to college. My link with the family had continued and grown, and I had often visited them, to talk with Linda and sometimes to babysit for her.

Linda's letter was brief but urgent. God had woken her up in the middle of the night, she said, and had given her a word of prophecy concerning me. The 'word of prophecy' consisted of a single sentence: *Come home, Jacqui*.

I read the letter with respect and some regret. It was as if Linda, because of our relationship in the past, was expecting that her letter would bring me home immediately.

But all my new commitment cried out in reply, that if she were only here with me in Houston – if she could only meet the people I was working with and study the teachings of Reverend Moon as I was doing – she wouldn't want to bring me back. *I wish Linda understood the reality of this*, I thought wistfully.

It was one of the costs of joining the Church. Those whom we loved wouldn't understand. I knew that; Reverend Moon had said so in his writings. I said a prayer for Linda, folded the letter carefully, and placed it in a trash bin.

8 DETROIT

Detroit: City (1978 est. pop. 1,245,000), SE Mich., on the Detroit River between lakes St.Clair and Erie. Detroit is a port of entry and a major Great Lakes shipping and rail centre. Its early carriage industry helped Henry Ford and others to make Detroit the 'automobile capital of the world' ... With the development of land and water transportation, the city grew rapidly during the 1830s. It assumed great importance after the mid-19th cent. as a shipping, shipbuilding, and manufacturing centre. In July, 1967, race riots in Detroit caused property damage estimated at $150 million.

[*The International Geographic Encyclopaedia and Atlas,* Macmillan Press, 1979.]

For three months we worked systematically through Houston, and we had still barely started. There were still whole areas to be covered, and we were only beginning to frame strategies appropriate for the different parts of the city.

For the enormous office complexes, for example, we changed product. There was building going on everywhere, great glass skyscrapers inhabited by big business deriving its income from oil. We went into the new office buildings selling foil etchings which, mounted on matching mats, framed and under glass, looked quite impressive. There were sets of Red Indian scenes, and one in particular that I had great success with was of Nell Gwynne's house in England.

They were flashy but attractive. If you held them to the

light at different angles you got different effects. One set was of antique cars of imitation gold foil. We did a roaring trade in these, and often a businessman would buy a whole set, to make his office look furnished.

I was learning salesmanship, tailoring the product to the market. I could have sold roses in the office blocks, but the pictures were much more acceptable. I was beginning to understand how to present my product, and the kind of introduction that was most effective. I was getting on well, and each day I earned large sums.

So it was a complete surprise when one day Sam said to me, without any warning, 'You've got a new mission.'

'New mission?' I queried, not understanding what he meant.

'That's right.' He was matter-of-fact, almost casual. 'You'll be leaving here.'

I gulped. 'Where will I be going?'

'Detroit.'

'When?'

'Tomorrow.'

'How many of us will be going?'

Sam paused. 'Just you, Jacqui. You'll be going on your own.'

My mission was, to be part of a team that would start a 'home church' in Detroit, and go out witnessing. Our purpose would be to bring others into the group. I wouldn't be fundraising at all.

I tried to have a positive attitude to Sam's announcement, and to show willingness; but I was torn between a desire to fulfil the new mission and at the same time to stay in Houston with Sam and the team. Though I had been in Michigan before and had passed briefly through Detroit on leaving the camp at Cheboygan, I had no idea what to expect and hardly any expectation of what it would even look like. But much more than that. I would be leaving behind me, for the first time, Sam who had brought me into the Unification

Church, and Louise, with whom I had become close through sharing good and bad times fundraising. I had made other good friends among our small team.

After less than six months, this latest departure was like a kind of growing up, like leaving home for the first time.

I said my goodbyes, and looked round the bungalow nostalgically for the last time – though I had seen very little of it anyway, because we had been working so hard. Sam gave me an envelope. 'You'll find your plane ticket in there, and the address you're to go to. There's a few dollars to cover things you might need on the trip, as well.'

Next day he drove me to the airport. We said goodbye, he gave me a brief hug and an encouraging smile. 'Don't worry, Jacqui, it will all be fine. Success to True Parents and their mission! – take care of yourself. We'll miss you.'

I never found out why I had been sent to Detroit. I had already discovered that people's movements within the Church were dictated almost arbitrarily; a phone call from New York, somebody returning from a distant workshop with instructions – and you could be uprooted and moved halfway across the country within a matter of hours. In the context of the work we were doing, it seemed entirely reasonable.

The day I left, Houston was hot, well up to its normal temperature of 102° in the shade. So that I would be comfortable on the plane, I wore a pair of lightweight nylon trousers, a short-sleeved blouse and a cotton jacket.

The flight was a direct one through to Detroit. I didn't take too much notice of what landscape was visible below me. My mind was churning as I contemplated the future.

The plane sank to rest on the runway, and I cleared the few formalities and was soon standing on the highway outside Detroit airport. There I had my first unpleasant shock.

None of us had thought about the difference in the climate

between Houston and Detroit, which was at that time in the grip of winter. I gasped as a chill wind bit into me. One or two passers-by looked curiously at me: a tall, oddly-garbed person shivering in thin summer clothes, standing among piles of snow.

After the shock of the cold came the second unpleasant realisation. I had assumed that the airport would actually be in Detroit, and that getting to the address I had been given would be a matter of taking public transport. But the airport was miles out of the city. I checked the money that Sam had given me. I had fifteen dollars. On a piece of paper enclosed with the money was a name I did not know – Sherry Wrightson – and an address which could be anywhere in Detroit.

A line of yellow cabs stood near by. I joined the queue. Eventually it was my turn. I tossed my small suitcase into the back and climbed in after it.

'Where to?'

The cab driver was large and affable. I pulled out the piece of paper with the address on it and showed him. He nodded, and swung out into the traffic. Soon we were speeding along an enormous highway.

'Sure is cold,' he grunted. I was suddenly uncomfortably aware how incongruous my clothes must look.

'I just flew in from Houston,' I explained. The cab was heated, and I sat back as my limbs began to thaw.

'Well it ain't Houston weather here,' he remarked. 'Bitter as hell today.'

I watched the highway unfolding before us.

'You English?'

'Yes,' I said. 'From Windsor.'

He swivelled round in his seat, a huge smile spreading across his face. 'Now I always wanted to go to England, you know that? London, that's where I'd want to go. You got so much in that little city ...'

As we talked about England I watched the taximeter out

of the corner of my eye. The dollars were mounting alarmingly.

'Are we in Detroit yet?' I asked.

He shook his head and launched into further praise of England. After a little while I stole another look at the meter. The fare had risen to twenty dollars.

'Scotland, now that's another place. I got Scottish relations, family back there, I'd really like to visit— '

I gathered my courage in both hands. 'Look,' I said, interrupting him in mid-flow, 'You'll have to stop. I've run out of money.'

He took his eyes off the highway and transferred his gaze to me. 'You mean you don't have any?' he asked severely.

'No. I've got fifteen dollars and I thought that would be enough ... Nobody told me it would be so far in to Detroit.' I flushed scarlet. 'I'm truly sorry,' I said lamely.

'Humph!' He scowled thoughtfully, and brought the cab to rest at the kerb. 'How much do you have, you say?'

'Fifteen.' I felt utterly helpless. I didn't even know whether he was deliberately taking me a long way round.

I told him the whole story, where I'd come from, where I was going. 'Do you think I could send you the money?' I pleaded. 'I just don't have it on me.'

He thought for what seemed ages. Then he grinned. 'OK,' he said, and revved the engine. 'OK, you send it me.' We moved out into the traffic again.

But the meter continued to soar, and before long I owed the driver forty dollars. 'Look,' I said. 'I think you should drop me here. I don't think you ought to take me any further. I've run up such a bill already. Are we in Detroit yet?'

'Yes,' he said, much to my relief. 'That's the Detroit River you see there. You're outside the Renaissance building. You sure you want to get out?'

'Sure,' I said firmly.

'It's twenty below,' he said doubtfully. 'You ain't dressed for it.'

'I'll be fine.' I gave him my piece of paper. 'Please write your address on the back.'

He scribbled a few lines. Then he looked again at the address I'd been given. 'That's about three miles away, down that way.' He handed the paper back to me. 'Good luck. Mind you send me them dollars.'

As I emerged from the warmth of the taxi the cold hit me so hard that I began shivering immediately. A keen wind whipped my face and hands, and I could hardly hold my suitcase. I stamped my feet to make them warm, but it did little good; I only had thin track shoes, and the freezing slush on the sidewalk was already penetrating them.

I made off at a brisk trot in the direction the cab driver had shown me, but after a few yards my hands were numb. I fumbled my suitcase open and found a pair of socks which I pulled over my hands in lieu of gloves.

The city was depressing, too. I had come from Houston, which was a bright, sunny, friendly place bustling with activity and prosperity. Here, I was walking down bleak winter streets where the shops all had steel mesh over the windows, and there were very few people about. I asked for directions once or twice, and the people I stopped were unfriendly.

I was walking in the direction of Wayne State University. After a while I left the city centre behind me, with its high-rise tenement blocks and office buildings, and entered a very run-down part of Detroit. As I picked my way past broken-down buildings, stepping over litter blowing along the street, I became more and more miserable. *Why am I here*? I thought bitterly. *I was doing all right in Houston. What am I doing here, Lord*?

Eventually I found the address I had been given. It was a flat in a large old house, and I climbed the stairs and knocked on the door.

There was no reply. Desperately, I knocked harder, but nobody answered. In the rest of the building I could hear muffled noises of people talking and the occasional door banging inside, but there was silence on the landing where I was waiting. I pressed my ear to the door. No sound could be heard from inside.

I opened my case and found another blouse, contemplated changing there and then, and finally pulled the new one on over the old. I sat on the floor, hunched over to keep warm.

I waited for three hours without moving, sunk deep in despair. Eventually I decided to go and look for Sherry. Clambering painfully to my feet, I shook the damp folds of my clothes free and went stiffly down the stairs and out to the streets.

Wayne State University campus was huge, and I had no idea who I was looking for. I didn't even know what faculty she was in or where to start looking. I wandered around for a while, occasionally asking students if they knew Sherry Wrightson, but nobody did.

It was growing dark, so I decided to walk back to the flat. It was still shut up. I would have burst into tears, except that I felt too dreary. Slumped down again at her door, I sat in a brooding, black depression until Sherry finally arrived an hour or so later.

'You're *soaking*!' A very tall black girl of about twenty-six dumped her bags unceremoniously on the floor and produced a key from her pocket. 'I'm Sherry, sorry I was out, what sort of trip did you have? I've been on campus, couldn't get out of it – come on in, dry out.'

I trailed in after her. Sherry flung off her thick coat and pulled off a woolly cap, shaking free a wild mop of hair. She sat down and awkwardly peeled off her boots. 'What *have* you got on?' she demanded. Then she peered at my shoes. 'Didn't you get a cab?'

'I didn't have enough money ... I walked in from the

Renaissance Centre. These are the only clothes I've got.'

'Well, we'll have to sort you out tomorrow,' she said briskly. 'I'll make you a hot drink now. Look, I keep my things in that closet over there – pick yourself something warm and come and sit by the fire.'

Twenty minutes later, wearing a chunky sweater and wrapped in a blanket, warming my bare feet at the fire and drinking a mug of scalding coffee, I began to relax. Sherry was an exuberant, talkative companion, and she was full of information about the plans for the new mission.

'In a week's time Gregory arrives,' she said. 'He'll be leader, and we'll set up a new centre.'

'Here?' I asked, looking round the attractive but tiny flat.

'No – I stay here, I'm with CARP.'

'What's CARP?'

'College Association for Research into Principle – we work among the college students. That's why I'm staying here, near campus. The team will find somewhere else. Then the hard work begins! Have you done witnessing before?'

'I was fundraising in Houston,' I explained. 'You know – roses, pictures, that sort of thing.'

'You'll find it a bit different now,' remarked Sherry. 'It's all witnessing from now on.'

During the week, Sherry was out of the flat a good deal, and I went with her when I could; but several times I found myself on my own, wandering round the college campus or killing time in the cheerless streets. I loved the college bookstore; its college atmosphere drew me like a magnet; and the students, dressed for winter in trendy padded down jackets, ski-wear and hiking boots, reminded me of the spirit of San Francisco. Occasionally I saw a student who looked like Sam, and then I remembered with intense clarity the freedom and fellow-ship of those early days.

Sherry gave me a sweater, and the day after I arrived she took me to the shops and bought me a coat; but I looked terrible. In Houston I hadn't had time to buy clothes – those I had were adequate, because it was so warm. I'd never had a problem with shoes, either; a pair of sneakers wore out in a fortnight with all the running one did, and I was provided with new pairs regularly. Yet I had never felt able to ask for anything, and I was very aware of the fact that I had nothing of my own nor the means to acquire anything. That was how it was in the family.

So for the few days I walked the streets in my thin shoes and thick coat with the sweater that didn't match, and I was terrified. The area around the university was in the heart of black Detroit, a part of the city which I was later to love, but which at first unnerved and frightened me. As I walked through its streets I found myself remembering American movies I'd seen, full of poverty and crime, and all set in similar surroundings. There had been disastrous race riots in Detroit ten years before, and there was still a heavy police presence. It all contributed to a – largely imagined – sense of brooding threat.

I felt desolate all that first week. To have first left San Francisco, and the happy environment there, and then to have left Houston, which had been a warm, friendly city, and now to find myself in Detroit, snowbound and vulnerable, was like a bereavement.

And then Gregory arrived, and matters immediately improved. He brought two others with him, Tony and Joseph, so there were four in our team. I liked all three of them immediately, and warmed to Gregory particularly, who had an air of authority combined with a very pleasant, friendly way of relating to people.

I knew from the outset that we would all work well together. I related most easily to Tony, because he was almost my own age, five years older than me; whereas Gregory was in his mid-thirties and Joseph was nearly forty.

When I was introduced to Joseph I recognised him. He had been at Camp K while I was there, leading the singing and working as a driver for one of the vans. He was a shy, remote man, and habitually wore the expression of somebody who had experienced terrible tragedy in life.

I was never quite sure what Sherry's position was. She had joined with four other black students five years earlier, when she met a witnessing team in Detroit. Of the five, two had full-time jobs and Sherry and two others worked with CARP. When our team became established, she didn't live with the rest of us, and she studied part-time at the university as well as working with CARP.

Her commitment was partial, and I had not come across such a phenomenon in my entire involvement with the Unification Church. She spent frequent weekends with her parents, and was quite different from the totally dedicated and committed people I knew in the Church. I found it hard to reconcile her lifestyle with all that I had read in *Master Speaks*, or the long discussions I had had with Unification Church leaders.

Within days Gregory had arranged to rent a beautiful flat for our team, just opposite the Renaissance Centre. It was part of a block of luxury penthouse suites, with white carpets, extravagantly thick-piled, throughout the entire apartment. We had almost no furniture – just a television and a video recorder, and a low table on which stood two marble Korean vases and a portrait of True Parents, Reverend and Mrs Moon.

The table was our altar. Each Sunday, at 5 a.m., we showered and put on our best clothes; then the girls sat on the right and the men on the left in front of the altar. We each had a card on which were printed the words of a statement called the 'Pledge', written in the form of a creed. We sang a song from a book called *Holy Songs*, and then recited the Pledge in unison.

Then we knelt, touched our foreheads to the floor, and stood up; this was repeated three times. By doing so, we were bowing to True Parents. This was followed by a period of corporate prayer, also in unison, lasting for one minute. Finally we knelt and prayed our own, private prayers, after which we would go back to bed and sleep for a few more hours.

I valued the Pledge service. It provided a note of ritual and ceremony which was otherwise lacking in the hardworking life of our small community. It gave us a sense, too, of sharing in a world-wide movement, even though we were in Detroit as struggling pioneers.

There were other aspects of Unification Church life which came to the fore now that we were in a home church situation and living in a small group. For example, Gregory taught us the use of 'Holy Salt', which was salt originally blessed by Reverend Moon. This had to be sprinkled over the food in a restaurant or any environment that needed to be purified and set apart for our use. If there was no Holy Salt available, in an emergency we could blow three times on the food. There were certain places where Holy Salt had been used to consecrate 'Holy Ground', and Reverend Moon himself had visited one spot in each State and blessed it. On one memorable day off, Gregory took us to Bell Island, ten miles out of Detroit, to the Detroit Holy Ground. To stand on ground which the Messiah had personally visited was a wonderful experience.

But such occasions were highlights. Life quickly fell into a pattern. Each day we had morning service, which was something we had never done in Houston. There our base had been a special fundraising centre for the California family. But in Detroit we were a home church, and worship assumed a larger place in our lives.

And after morning service, we went out to witness; and that was something altogether different from anything I'd done before.

9 WITNESSING

Your witnessing technique is the most important thing. Always think, How can I attract this person to me? There is only one method for doing this. That is the spirit of serving that person. When you are going to do something to take advantage of the person, that is an obstacle. But in serving the person you are brought closer together.

[Sun Myung Moon, *Master Speaks*, January 3rd, 1972.]

Witnessing meant trying to persuade people to come to our centre for a meal, in the same way that I had been invited by Sam, to hear more about the Unification Church.

I worked with Tony, who was an engaging companion. He was from an Italian background, and very tall, with a slight stoop. His hands were large and strong – the hands of a basket-ball player; when we had times of recreation, he was fond of fooling around with a ball.

We spent part of the time fundraising; each Friday and Saturday we bought product and sold it. But the money was not, as had been the case in Houston, sent back to San Francisco; it was kept by the home church in Detroit and used for our living expenses, food and accommodation. Then the rest of the week we went out witnessing.

Just as I had been taught to set goals for myself when fundraising, so we were taught, in Detroit, that we should have the goal of each winning three 'spiritual children' – converts to the Unification Church. Gregory encouraged us to strive for this goal with prayer, self-sacrifice, and unstinting labours.

The area that Tony and I were given in which to achieve it was Highland Park, a district outside the central city area. It was near the site of the original factories where Henry Ford had built his first cars, and which had been the lifeblood of Detroit for many years afterwards. The managers of the factories had lived well, in houses which still remained in the Park: sprawling buildings from another age, brick mansions and wooden ones with elegant verandas looking out on to large gardens.

But the wealthy whites had moved on long ago, out to the prosperous suburbs. Now the district was predominantly a black area, with a few older German and Polish families remaining.

In this area Tony and myself had 360 homes each which we were to visit. The plan was to take a questionnaire, with various conversation-provoking discussion-starters to help us. This would hopefully secure us at least a conversation on the doorstep. Having made an initial contact we would then go back later and ask if they would like to see a video at the centre. The video was of the *Divine Principle*, composed of some lectures given by Unification Church leaders.

We discovered that visiting homes took a long time. If you got talking to somebody it could be two or three hours before you moved on. And we had a wonderful time with the black community. Most of the old people watched endless religious television shows – a number of which were actually made in Detroit. Hardly any of them seemed to go to church, or indeed to leave the house very much at all; but most enjoyed a leisurely conversation about matters spiritual, and were quite reluctant to let us go.

Tony in particular loved to sit talking to people. One eighty-year-old lady lived alone in a house that reeked of garlic and glycerine. 'I got to this old age by chewing garlic every day,' she informed us, and though the smell made us want to retch, we were never able to pass her house without wanting to call and see her. However, I was very restless in her home; but Tony – perhaps because of his Continental background! – ignored the garlic and would sit with her for hours, running his great hands through his curly hair, pondering her conversation with almost painful concentration. She was sprightly for her age, and a God-fearing woman.

But we made little impact on anybody; nobody wanted to see the video, and we were rapidly falling behind the daily visiting rate we knew we would have to keep up if we were to make our goal of 360 homes each.

As for my goal of three spiritual children, I knew that I wasn't going to make that either. I had no confidence. I was tongue-tied, I was deeply aware of my relative newness in the Unification Church, and I didn't have the right kind of aggression. Tony was a very similar person to myself, and we both knew that we were not doing well.

Sometimes, sitting in lovingly polished drawing rooms with the grandmother or mother of a black family (the father was usually nowhere to be seen), I would despair of ever getting a word in, let alone of winning a convert. After my successes in fundraising, it was a major disappointment to me that I was not equally successful in witnessing.

The area was a mixture of quite wealthy families and appallingly deprived ones. We saw drug addicts, recognisable by lines of hypodermic scars up their arms; and sometimes we met with prejudice and dislike. As two young white people, we were regarded by some as a threat or at least an annoyance, and this further impeded our efforts. The least friendly families, in fact, were the white ones, who usually refused to talk at all. They seemed outraged that we should have assumed that they had any need to talk about spiritual matters to anyone.

But though there was a continuing undercurrent of

distrust, talking to people on their doorsteps and in their own homes was much more satisfying than the time we had to spend talking to people in the Renaissance Centre, which was also part of our 'beat'. Both Tony and I found it very difficult to initiate conversations.

Many people visited the Renaissance Centre on business or pleasure. Four huge towers rose above it, one a top-class hotel and conference facility, the others office complexes. The Centre itself was a multi-storey, very exclusive shopping plaza. The shops and restaurants were so grand that I never dared to go inside them. They showed every sign of prosperity, and their customers seemed to be few and very select.

I spent a great deal of time just watching people, trying to pluck up the courage to get them into conversation. Whereas only a few weeks before, I had been willing to approach bizarre-looking strangers and persuade them to buy a rose, now I was tongue-tied at the prospect of making conversation with perfectly ordinary businessmen and women.

We settled into a routine. In the mornings Tony and I took a bus out to Highland Park, and the first thing we did was to go to a MacDonald's hamburger bar. Every morning we were given money by Gregory to buy our food during the day. There was a 'condition' in the Unification Church at that time, that no member was allowed to eat breakfast. We were only permitted to have liquids. So we began the day with the largest milk shake they served.

Then we worked our way through however much of our quota of houses we could manage, and at mid-day we had lunch, which was always fish-burger and French fries, which I hated. In the afternoon we worked through to the early evening, and then went back to the flat by bus.

I got on well with Tony. Sometimes I felt that the only really effective thing I was doing was keeping his spirits up. He told me a great deal about his past, which was something that the Unification Church discouraged – we were supposed to put the 'things of old' behind us. But we were thrown together by our own inability to be effective witnesses, and we often had days when we couldn't face witnessing and would sit for hours talking instead. Then he would tell me about his days as a university dropout, when he'd chain-smoked marijuana, and how he had eventually met the San Francisco family just as I had done, and become a member of the Church. His hair had been long and was still thick and wiry; he had had it cropped short as a symbol of his commitment. But he had been a reluctant convert, an agnostic for a long time, and he marvelled at the way in which I had accepted the whole teaching right from the beginning.

We had good times together, and many laughs. But we were conscious, all the time, that we were not doing what we should be doing, that our quotas were far from fulfilled, and that we were just playing at witnessing. We never had an effect on a single person, I am sure. I don't think we got anywhere with anyone. All told, we managed to visit sixty homes between us in six months.

There were highlights. On one of our rare days off we went to a big firework display in Detroit, and we enjoyed that. There was a fortnight we spent with Gregory on an Illinois University campus, witnessing with others in what was called an 'International One World Crusade', and several people joined the church there as a result. For me, those two weeks recaptured the flavour and feel of the San Francisco family, and I left with a renewed sense of homesickness.

Back in Detroit, we seemed occasionally to be on the verge of a breakthrough, often enough to keep us going out day after day.

One contact, for example, was a married man who seemed very interested in the Unification Church. I went to visit him in his home later. He was a blues singer and bass player. I played guitar with him, and we talked, but it was obvious that he wasn't really interested after all. Another contact who really wanted to talk turned out to be a practising member of the Baha'i faith, who was as anxious to convert us as we were to convert him. We had a meal with him, and he was a very pleasant, sincere person. 'In the Writings,' he declared, 'it is said that there will be many great teachers.'

In fact he talked to us much more about his faith than we were able to talk to him about ours. He was very complimentary about our group, but his own beliefs were so open-ended that it was impossible to take him step-by-step through the *Principle* as we had planned. So once again we left, having had an enjoyable evening, but with nothing to show for it.

And all the time there was a sense of failure and incompetence that weighed us both down. We had been given a mission, we knew that it was important, but we really had no idea what we were trying to do.

I tried to cheer myself up by writing letters to Sam and the people at San Francisco.

Hi! We're settled in here at Detroit, we've set up the home church and we're out witnessing every day. If you've time please write and let me know how things are going with you ...

But none of the letters was ever answered. I told myself that it was because of the way that the Church was growing – there was no guarantee that people were still where I thought them to be. But I couldn't help wondering whether I was being ignored, or whether people were just too busy to reply. It made me feel forgotten, and that hurt, because it was the San Francisco family, with its warmth and closeness, that had first made me want to go into the Church.

Tony and I also found ourselves feeling depressed about our own role in the home church. Gregory had selected Joseph to be his assistant. Joseph, like Sherry, seemed to be on the fringe of things, without the 100 per cent commitment that I had come to expect everyone to have, even though he lived in the centre and shared everything with us. He and Gregory had their own mission, which was to get to know the local dignitaries and officials and present the Church to them. They were a kind of public relations team, and it was expected that they would also be witnessing to these elevated people.

Tony and I understood the need for this to be done, but it was very hard, coming home on the bus after a day of rebuffs and frustration, not to think that we had been cheated; that they had taken the comfortable and prestigious duties and left the difficult and dirty work to us.

And yet there was a closeness about our tiny community, at least between Tony and Gregory and myself, though our relationship with Joseph and Sherry was of a lesser degree. I quickly grew to love Gregory. He was full of fun, and was a great story-teller. He had a fund of stories about 'Father'. When I was depressed – which was quite often – he knew how to cheer me up; and, though physical contact between team members was frowned upon, Gregory often surprised me with an unexpected hug.

But it was a time dominated by a sense of guilt, a feeling that if I were only doing my job properly I would be achieving the results that everybody thought I ought to be achieving and which, indeed, everybody assumed I was, at least in terms of visits made. I used to think of Jessica and the others who had pioneered the work in San Francisco, and I would try to imitate them, but it wasn't working out.

Living in Detroit did not help. The city was facing massive unemployment, with layoffs in the car industry which was its main commercial activity, and in the suburbs and ghettoes in which we worked it showed. There was a prevailing gloom in many homes, and we came with a message of hope and nobody wanted it. It was a grinding, working-class culture, without the lifestyle that there had been in the West, and we had nothing that people needed.

Though I was always tired, I sometimes lay awake at night and wrestled with my own frustration. If I was doing so badly, why did I feel unable to talk to people about it? Why was there no obvious source of counselling? Gregory and Joseph were out all day just as we were, and Tony and I were only reinforcing each other's failure.

I knew that I needed help, and I was troubled. My letters to California remained unanswered, Tony and I continued to waste time, and I felt that I was going nowhere. I prayed sometimes, but nothing changed. I had long since stopped reading the Bible regularly – there simply wasn't time, and Bible studies in the sense I had known them in Britain didn't have a part in the Unification Church routines. I read *Divine Principle*, but gained little comfort from it. Gregory had a few copies of *Master Speaks*, but even these did not hold the encouragement they had when I had been a successful fundraiser in Houston.

My spiritual difficulties increased in a completely unexpected way when I received a letter from my mother. We had been corresponding intermittently since she had been to Camp K, and our letters had been deliberately bland and non-committal. I had said nothing in my own, infrequent letters home, about the frustrations and disappointments of witnessing. I'd stressed the warmth of fellowship, the interesting sights of America, and the excitement of working full-time in a Christian mission.

But now my mother was ready to tell me of the radical change that had come over her own life, and she had a great deal to tell me besides.

When she returned from Camp K and told Dad what had happened there, he had been bitterly upset. He became deeply depressed, and had times of seething anger, when he used to talk about going to Unification Church premises in Britain and burning them to the ground. My father is a peaceable man and would never have carried out his threat, but the very fact that he had made it was an indication of the strength of his feelings. He was very positive about Mum becoming a Christian, and even went to church with her occasionally; but his own feelings were dominated by his violent anger towards the Church his daughter had joined.

Mum herself, since her visit to California, was afraid of the Unification Church. She saw the leaders at Camp K as gaolers. She refused to attend the official parents' functions which the English family arranged for people whose children had joined the Church. They were informal occasions, designed to give information and to build relationships with parents, but neither of my parents wanted anything to do with them.

The effect of my joining the Unification Church, in short, had been to cast a cloud of resentment and bitterness over my parents' life. In their letters, though they gave no details, the bitterness had been evident for some time. I had talked to Sam about it, and he had counselled me not to lose heart.

'Pray for them,' he advised me, and I had done so.

But I had no knowledge whatever of the extraordinary things that God was doing in the lives of my parents.

Almost a year after committing herself to Jesus in San Francisco Mum had been to a meeting, near her home, of the Full Gospel Businessmen's Association. There she had experienced in a powerful and unmistakable way the peace of God, who had taken away her fears and resentment and replaced them with a deep and certain assurance that I was going to be under his protection.

She touched on this only briefly in her letter, for she wanted to tell me for the first time that she had become a Christian. But more than that: two months afterwards, Dad had also become a Christian, and God had transformed his attitudes and filled his heart with a spirit of forgiveness. So her letter contained two pieces of extraordinary news.

When I left home, my parents had no Christian commitment and rarely went inside a church. Now they were enthusiastic members of the church which I had abandoned.

The news only aggravated my spiritual discontent. Of course I was thrilled – hadn't I prayed for this very event to happen, day after day for years? But my parents' criticism was now much more sharply directed at the teaching I was receiving. Before, they had seen the Unification Church as a cult that broke up families and wasted young people's lives. Now, they knew Jesus for themselves, and scrutinised everything that I said about my own discoveries in the light of their own experiences. Dad in particular became an avid reader of any books he could find about the Unification Church, and his letters to me from then on were full of challenges and biblical arguments.

So the news that ought to have thrilled me beyond measure only added to my sense of frustration and restlessness. What made matters worse was that my options, as I saw them, were so limited. I couldn't contemplate leaving the Church, for to do so would have been to negate everything that California had meant to me. But I knew that unless things changed radically, I was going to have serious problems.

And then, six months after my arrival in Detroit, a new mission opened up, and things really did change radically.

10 MFT

Mobile team activities are like guerilla warfare; hitting one place, moving to another, attacking another, and moving on. We don't have any home base; from one day to another we are moving.

[Sun Myung Moon, quoted in Frederick Sonntag, *Sun Myung Moon and the Unification Church*, 1977.]

In one sense, there was an arbitrariness about the way my life in the Unification Church was developing. No reason was ever given for a particular move, as to why one person had been chosen rather than somebody else, or what gifts and abilities had been considered necessary in the new situation. The message came from outside, through one's leaders, probably from New York, though one never knew.

On the other hand, I gradually realised that other people in the Church were having very similar careers to myself, and a pattern became apparent which was confirmed when I asked my leaders about it. There was a formula for one's growth within the Church. It was based on the description of growth in *Divine Principle*, which says that everyone must begin in the position of a servant to servants, work at that role for a number of years, and then progress to being a servant. After serving in that way for a further period the next stage is to be an 'adopted child', and finally one attains the level of being a 'true child'.

I found these concepts hard to grasp, though I could see how they fitted with the Asian view of society and the strong element of service in that culture. While I was in the home church in Detroit, I had very little sense of service. Tony and I all too easily lost sight of any goals and faith that we were going to accomplish anything at all. It was a slow, difficult task, and I took little pleasure in it.

When Gregory announced that we were going to have one of our rare days off, the news lifted our spirits considerably. The Mobile Fundraising Team which was based in Detroit was having a recreation day and we were invited to join them.

Though I knew 'MFT' were working from Detroit, I'd not had anything to do with them and knew very little about them, apart from references in *Master Speaks* and passing remarks from the leaders. Gregory told me more.

'They are organised differently from ourselves and the California family,' he explained. 'They are headed up by Japanese teams, and the head of MFT himself is answerable only to Father.'

The link with Reverend Moon gave MFT a special glamour for me, and I looked forward to meeting them. We went to a park in Detroit, and just as we often did on days off, we had competitions and sporting contests.

There was actually a reason for this. 'You have to keep the fighting spirit strong,' I had been told. 'Fight against Cain! Inside you, Satan is struggling to have dominion over you, and you must resist him with all your strength.' There was a good deal of teaching like that, about evil spirits and the need to 'crush Satan'; physical exercise and competition were considered to be helpful in developing the right attitude.

A wrestling match was staged. It was Korean wrestling, where victory goes to the wrestler who can get his opponent outside the circle in which they both stand. I had never enjoyed physical sports. When I was younger I had been a hockey-player, and had found that very difficult because I didn't have the fighting mentality that made you cannon into people and bend the rules when necessary. On the other hand, I was tall, which gave me an advantage, and I was not slightly built.

When my name was called and the wrestling was due to begin I shook my head and decided to be a spectator. But Gregory squeezed my arm. 'Go out there and do your best,' he murmured. 'I'm sure you can win!'

So I took part, and I won. I was pleasantly surprised, and was even more so when everybody applauded and cheered.

I spent the rest of the day in a warm glow of achievement, and was sorry when it was time to go back to the flat.

The next evening Gregory had a telephone call from New York, and there was a long conversation. When he put the phone down he looked serious.

'Jacqui, Tony, can we talk?'

We followed him into another room in the flat, away from the others. We sat on the thick carpet; the room was bare of furniture.

'That was the New York family,' he said. 'I have some news for you. Tomorrow you'll be joining MFT.'

Tony and I looked at each other in mingled shock and delight. My own first reaction was one of relief, that the terrible deadlock of my ineffectual witnessing was to be broken. Tony said,

'Where will we be going, Gregory?'

'Royal Oak, the other side of town,' he replied. 'There are about fifty there already, you met them yesterday.'

I digested the news. It wasn't so bad, it wasn't as if I would be going several States away. I'd be in striking distance of the little family here.

Tony sighed. 'You'll be getting replacements for us, I suppose.'

Gregory shook his head. 'No. I've been moved on too. I have to go to start another home church.'

I was very sad to hear that. I knew, with a sombre

certainty, that I would not see Gregory again. Long afterwards, I heard that he had been matched but had been increasingly unhappy with his matching, and had subsequently left the Church and was living with a woman who was also no longer a member. It was as if a rock in the solid structure of the Unification Church had given way under me.

The Detroit MFT lived in a big house in Royal Oak. The girls slept in two upstairs rooms; the boys slept in the basement. The leader when I arrived was a Mr Fujo, whose wife was in Japan. When I first arrived I had to attend a workshop, and I realised immediately that MFT fundraising was a matter of total dedication, consuming all one's waking hours, at a level of commitment for which San Francisco and Houston had barely prepared me.

It was explained that we would be expected to set goals. Not just financial ones, but spiritual, internal goals. An internal goal might be, for example, to overcome pride, to persevere in hope, to be determined in all situations. We were taught at the workshop that it was up to us to achieve our own goals, it was a matter of our efforts. The setting of such goals was a way of producing the kind of characteristics which were pleasing to God. It sounded a daunting prospect.

Our attitude to our product would have to be scrupulous. We would be selling candy; if we ever ate any of the candy we would be depriving the people of the opportunity of giving to True Parents. And those who did contribute money were, by doing so, paying indemnity for their sins; so if we ever spent any of the money that we had raised, to buy ourselves food and drink, for instance, then we ourselves would become liable for the indemnity and pay the price of the sins that the money had covered.

In fact, if the person who had given money was a murderer or a rapist, we would be taking the burden of that man's sins upon ourselves if we spent so much as a cent of it.

The teaching at the workshop was characterised by a severe insistence on cause and effect, and because I was new to it it seemed almost oppressive. I realised that the honeymoon days of San Francisco and the warm, successful days in Houston had now gone for good, and I had entered on a new stage in my life.

Everything was done very professionally and thoroughly. We would be given badges which were decorated with the Unification Church symbol and bore its name; we would carry letters confirming our charity status, and leaflets explaining that the funds were going to various worthy enterprises.

There was a strong emphasis in the workshop on competition, and this struck a chord in my own attitudes. 'You are the freedom fighters,' we were told. 'You are the front line. It demands enthusiasm and zeal.'

Having just come from a situation where enthusiasm and zeal had been early casualties, I wondered how easy I was going to find it to regenerate those qualities. But I resolved that I was going to try my hardest. I would set goals and achieve them. This was a second chance. I wasn't going to blow it.

By nature, I have always been a competitive person, and not always in a particularly nice way. At college, for example, it had been very important to me to excel and be a higher achiever than anybody else. In San Francisco, I had had a distinct feeling of being more spiritual than others, of being a better member because I'd started from a more informed position.

Had I wanted to, there would have been no point in seeking counselling for this trait among the leaders. It would have been encouraged. Competitiveness means achievement; if you take pride in your position, you fight to maintain it. It's an incentive, which is what we were encouraged to have.

There was a curious smugness in the way we all discussed

pride as theoretically something to be abhorred – unservantlike – yet refused to recognise it in ourselves. I would then have thought pride to be the unjustified belief in one's own superiority. But in truth, I really did think I was superior in several respects and thought the belief was entirely justified.

On MFT I developed a kind of double-think, whereby I was in fact very secure and sure of myself but contrived to convince others I wasn't. Of course, I then wanted people to realise that in fact I wasn't as insecure as I looked, so I began seeking praise and reassurance.

That was why the wrestling match was so important to me; why, indeed, it remained as a source of encouragement and reassurance, for my first months in MFT. It had been a time when I felt, 'Yes, this is me; there is something in me which can rise above everybody else.'

At the workshop, the writings of Sun Myung Moon were quoted extensively. They urged us to greater and greater efforts. 'Father has compared our struggle to that of Abraham when he offered Isaac,' we were told. 'Imagine what it would have been like, if he had changed his mind and not obeyed God. That is what we are like when we fail in our external or internal efforts to maintain 100 per cent effort.'

It was a solemn warning. Nobody asked questions or tried to refute the argument. 'Throughout history mankind has failed to meet God's standards,' the leader said. His face and voice registered distress and pain, as he spelt out the application. 'But we too can make a sacrifice of ourselves, by giving of our sweat and our tears. We too can lay our own lives on the altar. We can – we must – strike our flesh, so that we can liberate the spirit.'

Suddenly he beamed, and his face was transformed like a winter landscape lit up by a burst of sunlight. 'Remember the ram? The ram that the Bible says was caught in the thicket? God provided it as a substitute. You see? MFT isn't like witnessing. We can't bring new members into the team from off the streets. But our offering of money, the money we raise on MFT, is a substitute for that. That's how Father describes it. It's like Abraham's ram.'

As the workshop proceeded I learned more and more of the MFT basis of operation. It was rooted in *Divine Principle*. Everything had to be earned; the doctrine of indemnity, which I had been taught when I first began fundraising, was taught very strongly here. Our sins, and those of our ancestors, had to be paid for. Our labours were indemnity that we were paying, for our own and for others' sins.

Following the discussion of Abraham's sacrifice of Isaac, we were taught the concept of 'conditions', a term I had often heard in the community but had never quite understood. Just as it was crucial that Abraham's heart should be in the proper state for him to be able to offer his son, and thereby for God to show mercy, so we too must have an openness both internal and external for God to act through and in us. 'Setting a condition' meant cultivating that openness, and you might do it by taking a cold shower, working longer hours than necessary, praying instead of sleeping, or in many similar ways.

The seven-day fast I had taken at Camp K had been setting a condition, though I hadn't known it at the time. I had merely been following the example of people I respected. But the victory over Satan I had achieved when I resisted the appeal to go home with my mother shortly afterwards had been God's response to that condition.

'And remember,' the leader warned us gravely, 'you will *always* know when you are cheating and failing to fulfil the condition you have set up. If nobody else knows, our Heavenly Father will.'

But setting good conditions, or achieving personal goals, or even paying indemnity for sin, were not matters for praise. If we didn't make a large amount of money, then it was our fault, and we were held responsible. If we did make a lot of money, it was not us but God who had achieved it. In creating a condition, we had merely made it possible for God to bless us through our own efforts – and he had done so.

I absorbed the teaching of those first days in MFT soberly and with some sense of heaviness. When the workshop was over, I began work on one of the MFT teams. Those first days were very difficult. I'd had experience of fundraising, but never in such a dedicated and unrelenting context.

The teams were made up on the basis of how many people could fit in a van, and ranged between three and nine people. MFT had a big maxi Ford and General Motor vans, which would normally seat fifteen; and the whole of the back was used for product. There was a casket cool-box in each van to hold food and ice.

We rose early and came home late. Each day we had morning service in the van, where the importance of goals was re-emphasised. There was no day of rest, much less of worship. We worked all of every day, with only an occasional break. The sports day in the park, I discovered, had been a very special concession indeed. Once a month we would have a day off for recreation and an expensive meal out, or we would finish early and go to a movie. On such days we were given some personal spending money with which to buy gifts for parents, or new clothes. Afterwards we went back to the house in Royal Oak and collapsed into blissful sleep. But it was a concession, not a right.

It never occurred to me – as it would certainly have occurred to me only twelve months earlier – to question the fact that an organisation that described itself as a church should have any section of itself living as if Sunday were irrelevant. We were taught that the work we were involved in was too important for us to rest one day in seven.

'What we are doing,' we had been told in the workshop, 'is this: we are involved in God's work, we are restoring creation. In the beginning, God rested, but he has never ceased from his attempts to restore man since the fall. Nor should we.'

The restoration of creation, I knew well by now, was going to involve paying a great deal of indemnity. Sometimes the knowledge almost crushed me. Shackled by an overwhelming sense of my own sinfulness, I knew that I would have to work incredibly hard to pay for it all. I could readily understand why it was necessary to work on Sundays. In fact, I sometimes wondered whether a lifetime would be time enough.

11 IN THE FRONT LINE

When our life on this earth is completed, the record of how
we lived will become the measure for how much heaven
we deserve. This will be the standard: the love you unsel-
fishly bestowed upon your fellow man; the service you
willingly rendered for the benefit of others; the sacrifice
you courageously offered for humanity and for God. The
sum total of these deeds will become your treasure for
eternity.

[Sun Myung Moon, *God's Way of Life*, 1974.]

'Your area is from this street here, down through here, and
across to this junction here,' said Stephen. He had a
highlighter pen, and marked the streets up carefully for me
on my map.

Stephen was my team leader, and he was very meticulous.
He was in his early thirties, a short, studious-looking man
with blonde hair and gold-rimmed glasses. 'You'll be
partnering Rachel,' he told me.

Rachel was another recent arrival on MFT. She had joined
the Church as a result of the International One World
Crusade in Illinois which Tony and I had been on, and
joining MFT marked the end of her 'honeymoon period'.
She was English, and feeling homesick. She had been
delighted to find that I was English – I didn't sound English
at all. Living with Americans, I had picked up many of their
characteristic phrases, and my speech had developed the
beginnings of an American accent.

We smiled at each other. Stephen continued, 'You'll be in a residential area. Talk to people in the street, and don't be afraid to knock on doors. People are coming back from work, you'll find some opportunities if you press for them.'

Stephen carefully replaced the cap on his highlighter, slid it into his shirt pocket, and methodically buttoned the flap. 'OK, let's say two hours. No, two and a half. Jacqui, what's your goal for this area?'

'Sixty dollars,' I ventured. I had agonised a great deal about what I should set as my first goal. On one hand I had done well in Houston and twenty-four dollars an hour wasn't very ambitious by those standards; on the other hand, my previous efforts at fundraising, two days a week from home church, hadn't been very promising. So I struck a judicious balance at sixty dollars.

'Right, Jacqui. And Rachel?'

'My goal's fifty.'

'Fine – let's go for it, everybody.'

Rachel and I and the other team members loaded ourselves up with cases of peanut brittle bars, which was the product we were selling. Stephen dropped us at the start of our area, and we were left. 'See you later,' shouted Stephen, as the van pulled away.

It was a mainly residential area. I looked at Rachel and she looked at me. 'So how shall we organise it?' I asked her.

'Dunno ... How about taking separate sidewalks? I'll go up the other side and you stay here,' offered Rachel. 'Whichever of us gets to the intersection first can wait for the other to catch up.'

'That's a good idea; let's do that,' I agreed, and watched her cross the quiet street. I held my box of candy at a confident angle and set out.

A man was walking towards me, still fifty yards away; dressed in a suit, swinging a briefcase, he looked approachable and affluent. I went to meet him. 'Would you like to buy some candy, sir?' I asked.

'Whatever for?' he growled.

I fell back on a well-tried routine.

'It's two dollars for one bar and three dollars for two,' I said, trying to make it sound a terribly exciting offer.

'Never eat candy; and if I did, I can get it cheaper.'

I fished in my pocket for the card that I had been given. 'Here's some details of why we're selling it, sir. We're a charitable organisation.'

He did not take the card but peered down at it. Then he looked carefully at my badge, and snorted.

'*Moonies*!' he grunted. 'I wouldn't give a cent to that fascist! He's already a millionaire. Bug off!' He strode off, scowling.

I was extremely disheartened. There was nobody else on my sidewalk. Across the street I could see Rachel in conversation with an old lady. Lucky Rachel, I thought. Near by was the entrance to a block of apartments. I went in.

The hallway was dark and wood-panelled, and a porter's kiosk stood near the entrance. I approached it cautiously and asked whether I could sell candy to the residents. The porter grinned.

'That,' he said, pointing to a chrome pin on his lapel, 'is my badge. Now why d'you think I was given that badge?'

I smiled weakly. 'You tell me,' I suggested.

'To remind me of my job,' he said smugly. 'Know what my job is, young lady? It's to intercept people like you and stop them bothering the residents.'

'Couldn't you look the other way?'

'More than my job's worth,' he declared forcefully. 'More than my job's worth. "No soliciting", that's the rule, and that means you clear out. Now.'

Outside, a middle-aged woman was approaching. I held out my box forlornly.

'Would you like to buy some candy? It's one for two dollars and two for three dollars ...'

'What organisation are you with?' Her voice was raspy and her eyes peered like gimlets.

'We're a group that helps young people,' I said, and reached for the card again. 'It's called the Unification Church.'

Taking the card, she held it close to her face, scanning it slowly. 'Uh-huh – a church ... young people ... farming ... Well, that all seems in order. Now ...'

She opened her purse and handed me a five-dollar bill. I looked at it in disbelief and began frantically counting out candy bars.

'No, no, no,' she exclaimed impatiently. 'I don't want your candy. It's a donation, for your work.'

Thank you, God. I sent a prayer of gratitude heavenwards. I already had five dollars towards my goal, and I'd only been working a few minutes. I set off with renewed enthusiasm. As I walked I began muttering under my breath, *Fifty-five to go! Fifty-five to go!*

At the intersection Rachel was waiting for me. 'How did you get on?' she demanded. I showed her a handful of money. 'Sixteen dollars!' I reported. Rachel smiled. 'I made eleven,' she replied. 'It's going to be all right, I think.'

I suddenly remembered the man I had approached first. 'Rachel,' I said hesitantly, 'have you ever heard the word "Moonie"?'

Of course we knew nothing of the massive publicity that the Church was receiving in the popular newspapers on both sides of the Atlantic; we saw no newspapers anyway. If we had, stories of brainwashing and kidnapped teenagers would have seemed absurd.

Rachel laughed. 'Have I ever!' she said. 'You mean you really don't know it? It's what people call us.'

'That's what I guessed ... It seems a bit harsh, doesn't it? I just never heard it before.'

Rachel considered. 'Well, I was angry when I first heard it, but my leader explained that Reverend Moon has said that it doesn't matter; we should embrace people's antagonism and turn it into friendship; if they want to call us Moonies, we should accept it joyfully. I must say,' she added, 'I never thought much about it. Why did you ask just now?'

'That man I went to first – he seemed to know all about us.'

'Odd,' said Rachel carelessly. 'Maybe he'd met somebody witnessing.'

But it was not long before we discovered that we were in a district that had been worked by another team less than a month ago. Several people swore at me when I approached; one threatened to call the police, and in another tenement block somebody grabbed me by the scruff of the neck and pushed me back out on to the street.

'Three weeks ago, I had you lot round,' a grizzled pensioner stormed at me. 'Think I'm made of money?'

Later we arrived at the pick-up point, and the van was waiting.

'How was it?' asked Stephen.

We had both achieved our goals; I had exceeded mine by about twelve dollars, Rachel by two. Stephen took the money and placed it almost reverently in a container set aside for the purpose. 'Why don't you pray,' he said, 'and make your offering complete? Ask God to receive this money as representative of the people's sin, and to purify them.'

We prayed, a brief utterance of a few sentences. Then we flopped on to the van seats and poured out everything that had happened. As we talked, other members passed us hamburgers and other lovingly prepared food.

Stephen listened carefully, asking us to repeat some details. When I described the man I had spoken to first, he nodded sympathetically. 'You see, Jacqui, because we're based in Detroit and this is where our teams train, you'll find that often you aren't the first team to work in an area.'

He was counting the money, characteristically smoothing crumpled banknotes flat, turning them all the same way and slipping $50, $100 and $500 bank wrappers round the wads of notes. He sorted the coins into neat piles of different denominations. 'So now you have some new goals,' he added.

'New goals?' I paused in mid-munch.

'Yes – internal ones. All the people who treated you badly today, all those who swore at you, those who threw you off their premises – you have to forgive them. That's your internal goal.'

'It's awfully hard to think of doing that,' protested Rachel.

'Well, they can't help the way they treated you. They live under the same pressures that you are learning to overcome. Make it your goal. Forgive them.'

After I had been with MFT for a few days I began to work longer hours, and in a matter of weeks I was a full member of the team. I began to understand what 'mobile' meant in 'Mobile Fundraising Team' – there were always two or three teams working in various areas of Michigan, around the big university campuses or in the north of the State, and we had to be ready to travel anywhere, at a moment's notice.

Working days followed a strict routine. We got up at seven o'clock, and then had about ten minutes to get ready to go out. To be ready in time meant that twenty girls shared a bathroom, and the loo was in there as well; everything was totally public, and the lack of privacy was quite a shock at first. The bathroom was spotlessly clean – two people, a man and a woman, worked as housekeepers while the teams were out. But I often thought, scrambling for a place in the early hours of the morning, how nice it would be to have the room to myself for a few hours, to soak in the bath at my leisure.

When we had washed, the next task was to tidy up the dormitory. We slept in sleeping bags on the floor; these had to be rolled up and everything neatly put away. Only a few minutes were allowed for this, and we were expected to be downstairs and in the van very quickly.

As soon as we arrived at the van we started our allotted

tasks for the day, which had to be completed in ten minutes. One's task might be to clean the windows, or the inside, or perhaps to make sure that the van's stock of product was adequate – being 'on product' meant doing a rapid stocktaking and replenishing any low stock from the general store in the house. Finally we all got into the van.

The aim of the whole routine was to be on the road within a quarter of an hour of waking up. There was no time at all for private prayer, still less for make-up, or anything like that. There was no need to choose what we would wear; apart from underwear, the most any of us owned was two changes of clothes and a dress for Pledge service.

We showered each night on our return, and did our laundry once a week. In the mornings everything was geared to a quick get-away, and there wasn't even time to say a quick prayer in all the flurry.

As we drove to our area, we had morning service in the van. We took it in turns to have the responsibility of leading the worship. Whoever it was would read from *Master Speaks*, and say something about it. You might do some teaching, or share experiences you had had fundraising.

After the reading, we all prayed together, simultaneously for three minutes at the top of our voices. This was a method of prayer that was often used in the Unification Church, but it had an added function as we roared our devotions in the van speeding through the streets – it kept us awake. We averaged four hours sleep a night, and most of us were terribly drowsy in the van. I saw several heads nodding each morning. I was so bad at staying awake I found that the only way to manage was to stand up in the van, wedged against the roof to stop me falling over. Other people on the team used to thump each other on the shoulders and flail their own bodies to try to stay awake.

It was sometimes a frightening spectacle; a group of people chanting at top volume, hitting themselves and each other, some shaking their heads from side to side and punching their legs. Indeed, we were taught that we were at those times most vulnerable. We were trying to dedicate the day to God, we were 'setting a condition' in which we would be freeing God to work; and because of that, evil forces were attacking us all the more strongly. If we started off badly it could affect the whole day.

We had breakfast at the ubiquitous MacDonald's, usually a drive-in, where we ate either the standard breakfast of sausage, 'hash browns', egg and muffin, or a stack of pancakes with butter and maple syrup. (On MFT we were not bound by the condition which allowed only liquid breakfasts, and my vegetarianism was an early sacrifice to MFT work – eating fast food in hamburger bars meant we could spend more time fundraising). 'To go?' the server would enquire, and would pass us our food in polystyrene boxes. While we sat in the vehicle, waiting in the queue, we talked about the area we were going to that day, and we would announce our spiritual goals for the day.

Then it was time to collect a box of product and be dropped off, and the day's fundraising would begin. For most of the day we concentrated on businesses and factories, gaining entry on some pretext and systematically working our way through the staff. Between businesses, we ran. Everybody ran while they were fundraising; it was part of the fight against negativity. At the end of the morning we met up with the van again, counted up the money we'd made, and before doing anything else prayed and offered up the money and the work we'd done to God.

Lunch was either eaten in the van, or we would drive to the nearest fast-food bar. For eating in the van, Stephen provided highly nutritious home-made sandwiches. In the fast-food bars he bought us fruit juice instead of fizzy drinks, and he made us eat lots of fresh fruit as well as burgers. Unique among team leaders, he never joined in the stampede for fast food. The wholesome food was one reason I loved being on Stephen's team.

Afterwards, for about twenty minutes, we prepared our next batch of product, talked to our friends on the team, and then went back to work – either returning to the area we'd worked that morning, or going on to a fresh one. This would occupy us for another two or three hours.

Towards half-past five the business closed, and we would go to the residential, door-to-door areas. We knocked on doors and worked through blocks of flats until nine or ten o'clock, when we stopped to eat together. Afterwards we went bar-blitzing until one or two in the morning. If we were in an area where there were not many bars, some of us would be dropped outside an all-night drugstore or cafeteria, but we preferred bars because we invariably made more money from them.

Between one and two in the morning we were picked up, and counted up our money. We had to keep an account of what boxes of product we'd used and how much money, if any, we had spent – sometimes we were given money for lunch rather than meeting up at the van, and this money, because it had been specially 'blessed' – put aside for our use – had to be scrupulously accounted for. All receipts had to be produced for food and drink bought through the day.

Then we had an evening service, when many of us were as drowsy as we'd been in the morning one, though we were all expected to share with one another how we had got on during the day. Those who had failed to meet their goals repented publicly before God, and those who had, gave thanks; and all the money was once again dedicated to God.

Back at the centre we stumbled into bed between two and three o'clock. In the street outside, somebody was tidying up the van ready for the next morning. At seven, we would be up and out again.

Weekends meant extra work. On Friday and Saturday nights we were usually working until three or four in the morning, and it took at least an extra hour to count the money and tidy everything up afterwards. On Sundays, as a concession to the extra work, we didn't start until nine or ten in the morning. We also had a longer Sunday service, but we still went out and worked. At this time I made a personal commitment to write to my parents at least once every month; the letters were written in odd moments of relaxation at weekends, and painted a glowing picture of my new work.

The businesses closed on Sundays, so we went door-to-door selling all day. We never made as much money on Sundays as we did on other days, and we were allowed to set lower goals. Often we finished early and were able to go out for a meal. On the other hand, if we'd had a bad week, we were expected to make Sunday a day of reparation, when we worked extra hard to make up for the poor results in the week. Sundays like that were gloomy occasions, when we laboured under a sense of guilt and failure that was all the more crushing because we knew that Stephen was too kind-hearted ever to try to make us feel as guilty as we deserved.

It was a very punishing workload, but I had no problem in handling it. One reason was that my body tolerated the pressure, probably because my adrenaline saw me through. Another was that I was mentally and spiritually in top gear. In home church I had been unsuccessful, with no standard to aim for and a goal that was impossible from the start; now I was in a team, with a structure and a constant reinforcement from my fellow-members.

Most of all, I had a clear purpose in fundraising. I was on MFT. We were on the front line. Reverend Moon had told us so, and had urged us to sacrifice ourselves so we could serve others. He had told us that if we loved America more than the American people did, then we had the right to restore it, to claim back for God the offering that America was going to make.

With such a spiritual goal, the long hours and aching feet were all worth it.

12   PRESSURES AND PRODUCTS

Because of the fall ... mankind has not been able to realize [the Kingdom of God]. Instead, man has brought about a world of sin and has fallen into ignorance ... To restore fallen man back to his originally intended state, the new truth should be able to reveal to him his ultimate destiny in the course of restoration by teaching him the original purpose for which God created man and the universe. Many questions must be answered by this truth.

[The Unification Church, *Divine Principle*, 2nd edn, 1973.]

'You can have one pack for two dollars or two for three dollars.' I repeated my well-worn ritual sales pitch, and waited to see whether it would do the trick again. The sunlight streamed in through the office windows. Most of the typists were sitting in a semi-circle watching the secretary and me.

The girl was about twenty-four, vivacious, and pretty in a very petite way; I'd singled her out as a likely purchaser when I walked into the office, part of a suite in a grimy block by the Detroit River. She picked up one of my bars of candy and looked at it critically. 'Free samples?' she said teasingly. I blushed, unsure what to say. The other girls in the spacious, well-lit office tittered as they watched my embarrassment.

I had been taught that my product was totally precious.

Dreadful warnings had been issued to me about the spiritual consequences that would follow if I helped myself to one bite of the candy. Now, before my horrified eyes, she peeled the paper off one corner and licked the candy inside experimentally. Her eyes held mine with a smile.

'Hey, it's *nice!*'

She put her hand in her pocket and produced two dollars. 'There y'are, I'll take a pack!'

With a great sense of relief I watched the other girls throng round and clamour to buy my product.

It did not end there; other secretaries and typists came in from adjoining offices. I discovered that I'd called at the time that somebody would have been going to the local store for the coffee-break candies and cookies that everybody had ordered, so I had a ready-made market. One or two of the bosses came in to see what all the fuss was about, and I even sold some candy to them. By the time their coffee-break was over, I had sold my entire stock.

It was the kind of success one strove for in fundraising, not simply because of the amount of goods shifted, but because it was an oasis of welcome in a day that otherwise had its good times and its bad times.

I was learning the tricks of my new trade. It was hard work, harder than I had ever known before. Already I was learning that to be a successful fundraiser one had to generate custom, and make people really want to buy. Selling candy, there was a limit to the amount of money you could earn in a day, because we were selling the candy itself for only a few dollars; so that meant making lots of sales to make one's goal, such as when I had a good reception in an office block; and it also meant asking for donations from people.

I began to recognise patterns of response in people. I hardly ever met anybody who, having acknowledged me pleasantly, did not go on to buy something from me; and I met many whose reaction to my approach was extremely unpleasant, and sometimes I was met with loud abuse; I knew immediately that my best efforts were not going to charm them, and I wasn't going to sell any product there.

The days of a sixty-dollar daily goal were very quickly left behind as I adjusted to working the long hours that being on MFT involved. We were expected to make a goal for a whole month, so that for the first month I had to make sixty dollars every day. On the first day of each month we all had to set our goals, and I was fascinated to see the various factors that influenced the decision. The really brave fundraisers would always raise their goals even if they had had an unusually good month already. The more cautious would take into account such factors as whether the team was going into an area that had only recently been fundraised, or one in which it had had no success previously.

But whatever our reasoning behind setting the goals, we took the goals themselves immensely seriously. Nobody contemplated setting a ridiculously high goal, because not reaching one's goal was seen as a terrible failure.

'On the other hand,' Stephen told me, 'you must stretch yourself all the time. Do you want to go on making sixty dollars a day for ever? Father wants us to improve all the time, to reach people and help them in this way.'

'What should I set as my goal?'

'Well – I guess that, by now, sixty dollars comes fairly easy to you. You don't have any trouble making that. So why not aim for a hundred next month?'

The element of achievement was important, and it added a certain zest to the daily work. Some days I made my goal comfortably, some days I did miserably, and quite often I would double it. But however well or badly I did, the next day I had to start again at the beginning. That made it exciting.

In the home church situation I had had little encouragement and a great deal of frustration. In MFT, I found myself rising to the challenge and relishing the praise and encouragement when I did well. And all the time I reminded myself that it was not just a matter of cash; my work was having an effect in people's lives.

For that reason as much as any other, I became fascinated by success in fundraising. All of us on the team did. Rachel was fast becoming an accomplished fundraiser, and we helped each other; I tried to show Rachel the importance of 'loving America' and even gave her tips on American pronunciation.

The most inspiring thing for me at that time was being with the other team members, most of whom were making a lot of money. I made myself a permanent nuisance, demanding 'How do you *do* it? Do you have a particular attitude to fundraising? What's the secret?'

I had worked to acquire traces of an American accent; now I worked even harder at cultivating it systematically. I strove to lengthen my vowels, listening to other people's speech and carefully repeating it to myself when alone. I read aloud from *Master Speaks* in an amateurish Detroit snarl, which after a month or two became quite convincing. I wanted to be like my team-mates in every possible way. They were good fundraisers; with an urgency that would have surprised me had I seen it myself during the home church months, I dedicated myself to being like them. And there was another advantage in sounding like an American. My visa had now expired and I was illegally resident in the United States. But because I looked and sounded American, I was able to avoid being found out.

The goals were everything. You were always working towards them. To reach your goals consistently, both internal and external ones, demanded a level of commitment that was new and challenging. I learned a great deal of the nature of that commitment from watching a girl with whom I became quite friendly, called Sarah Goldberg.

Sarah was a mountain girl, who had rejected her wealthy Reformed Jewish background. She had left home after a difficult family break-up and had gone to live in the Colorado mountains in search of God and serenity. Climbing in the mountains one day, she'd had a terrible fall from a fifty-foot cliff. She escaped death by a miracle, but it took the skills of Colorado's top plastic surgeon to remodel her face.

The surgeon did a brilliant job and saved her from permanent disfigurement. But nobody would ever have called her stunningly attractive. Nor did she have a particularly dynamic personality to compensate. In truth, she seemed to have very little going for her. But she made a lot of money.

'How do you do it, Sarah?' I asked her, quite early in our friendship.

Sarah looked vague. 'Uh – I guess I try to think the right things.'

'What *are* the right things?'

'Well – like there are the basics, you know, you have to have the right things go through your mind, so you start by keeping your money goal right there in front of everything. You just don't ever forget it. It's kind of like having a picture on the windscreen of an auto – whatever you see, you see past that picture.'

Sarah was a quiet person by nature – her success as a fundraiser was a perpetual surprise to me – and she did not usually hold forth on any subject. As she talked about fundraising, however, her face lit up, she became animated, and she talked at length.

'Say your goal works out at twenty dollars an hour. Every hour you want to make twenty, right? So after a while you make two dollars. OK, then you look at your watch. You've got fifteen minutes left of that hour. So you say to yourself, "Now my goal isn't twenty an hour, it's eighteen in fifteen minutes." That's your new goal. And you go for it.'

I groaned in mock despair. 'You make it sound easy, Sarah. I'll never get it together.'

She scowled, half-humorously. '*That*'s why you find it difficult, Jacqui. You just let that negativity right into your head. You have to push it out, all the time. You have to shut out everything like that, and put it behind you, and concentrate like crazy on that goal.'

She looked at me seriously. 'It's not just goals and money in the bag, you know that, that's not what it's about. It's for True Parents' mission, it's preparing the way for the Lord of the Second Advent. God has been let down so often. I'm not going to let him down again. That's what it's all about, Jacqui. That's the mission.'

'Yes,' I agreed thoughtfully. 'That's what it's all about, I guess.'

When Sarah talked about fundraising in that way, her face changed and she radiated an internal strength and beauty that was unnerving.

She was a very special member of the team. We felt that God had saved her life so that she could re-dedicate it to him and serve and love the Messiah. I think we all drew strength from her.

As I tried to apply the principles of successful fundraising as expounded by Sarah and others, I became an extremely determined person, very competitive and not easily distracted. I became immersed in my work; hurtful things just rubbed off me and left me unscathed.

Except, that is, for the bad days. Even in the very earliest days on MFT, I had lapses into depression and frustration. Then, I lost my carefully cultivated concentration and things began to get through to me. I would start to find myself thinking, 'Oh, there's no use, I can't make *any* money today.' On days like that, if people swore at me my reaction would be 'Well, I'm going to swear right back at them! I'm going to kick their door down!'

When the bad days came my mind was full of sharp-tongued abuse. I went about my work framing vicious insults in my head, waiting for a victim. On days like that I couldn't just respond to rejection with a smile and a lighthearted 'Have a nice day!' When I was 'on-centre', that meant 'God bless you anyway!' or even – depending on the attitude of the person who had refused – 'I won't give up even if you kick me in the face!' But on the bad days, every insult I received, every unkind look, went straight to my heart and festered there.

On such days I realised that I was having to confront a side of my nature which was really unpleasant – the ability to see red, to want to act violently, to stop in my tracks and shout at somebody. I had never had to face up to such a problem before. I'd always been very contained and cool, and I never used to let my anger take control of me.

It seemed that the efforts I was making, the new motivation and commitment, were uncovering very nasty parts of my personality, and I had to deal with them. Sometimes I was successful, but other times I was not. Part of me wanted to conform and do what was expected of me; but another part of me hated it, and I resented having to do as I was told. There were times when I just refused to work. When I was in an apartment building I sometimes became so rebellious that I would find an empty stairway or utility room and fall asleep there, or sit fuming in resentment. Then as it neared the time I was due to be back at the van, I would start to feel guilty and begin to work frantically in an effort to belatedly catch up on my goal.

Sometimes I flopped into my sleeping bag in the early hours of the morning, tired out but unable to sleep. *I'm in God's place at God's time*, I told myself. *But why is it so difficult? Why do I have to concentrate so much, just to keep my temper? It wasn't like this in England ...*

After I had been on MFT for six months there was a change in the Detroit leadership. A Mr and Mrs Fujama arrived. They had a very tiny baby and a two-year-old son. It was unusual to have a family unit like that in the Unification Church – most of the married people I had met had been separated, with the husband and wife spending most of their time working for the Church in different parts of the world. I'd admired such dedication, but had missed the sense of a family environment.

Mr and Mrs Fujama's arrival helped me as I adjusted to life on MFT. Mrs Fujama especially was a very understanding woman, and I found her easy to talk to. Gradually I began to settle down and sort myself out; but the bad days never entirely went away, however much I tried.

The range of product we sold was varied. I began by selling candy and peanut brittle, but by the time the Fujamas arrived I had been moved on to other products. I moved on from candy to badges, which we sold for three dollars each. They were based on cartoon characters like Mickey Mouse and Donald Duck, and were very easy to carry around. We displayed them on boards covered in black velvet, and they looked very attractive.

From badges I was moved to more expensive jewellery, which was a much more profitable line because correspondingly fewer items had to be sold to make a certain goal. The pieces I was selling were gold-filled and solid silver necklaces, and some 9 carat gold jewellery. They sold for sixty or seventy dollars. By then my goals had risen accordingly, and I was making a great deal of money; each evening, as we counted up our takings in the van and offered them to God, I was always the top fundraiser of the day, or at least in the top two or three.

I was fulfilled and happy, at least for most of the time; and on the bad days, there was always Mrs Fujama's shoulder to cry on.

13 THE RISE

We are tigers to shake the whole world. We are great personages to change the whole world. Our stage is the whole world. The leading nation of the whole world is America and we want to shake America first.

[Sun Myung Moon, *Master Speaks*, November 10th, 1974.]

Over a year passed. I lost track of individual weeks and days. Very little of the outside world affected us; we had no time for newspapers or television, and we read no books or magazines apart from *Divine Principle*, *Master Speaks*, and other Unification Church publications. World events came and went, but we took little interest. In Moscow, the Olympic Games took place and many nations boycotted them; in Iran, fifty American hostages waited long months for their release; in Washington, President Carter's administration entered its final phase; and in California, a State Governor who had been a famous film actor in his day was mounting a presidential election campaign that would eventually put him into the White House.

In the Detroit fundraising centre the most significant development from my point of view was the arrival of a new product so attractive, so cheap to manufacture and so profitable to sell, that it became the most successful product of all: the wooden rose.

The boxes in which the new flowers arrived were small cardboard ones, each holding twenty-four blooms, and quite different from the large coffin-shaped polystyrene boxes of fresh roses that we used to collect from the airport in California and Houston. These needed no packing in ice. They were a quite different product. They were made of wood shavings, bound together and coloured and then soaked in glycerine so that the wood became very soft and curled like the petals of a real rose. They came on wires covered in green wax, so that they could be bent into attractive positions, and had artificial leaves which looked quite authentic.

They did not have the luxurious soft feel of the best artificial silk flowers, but they were really nice to touch. We dipped them in rose oil to give them fragrance. After they had been in a centrally heated air-conditioned office for a month, they looked terrible – faded, dried-out, papery and odourless; but straight out of the packet they looked beautiful.

They cost us about forty cents, and we sold them for six dollars each. If we were working a wealthy area we sold them for even more – seven or eight dollars. We were very flexible, changing our prices depending on where we were and how well they were selling. Sometimes we would even sell them for five dollars each if necessary; and we were always ready to negotiate a good price if somebody wanted to buy a quantity.

We were inventive in marketing, too; we sold handblown glass vases with them, tall slim test-tube-like vessels. One arrangement which was the most popular I sold was three flowers in a double-stemmed, heartshaped vase. It sold for twenty dollars, and so I only had to sell five and I'd made a hundred.

I changed my sales patter as the new product got under way. We were taught that selling product was so important in the work of the Unification Church, and the implications so significant in the life of the person to whom you were selling, that the end justified extreme means. Those of us who attended that initial MFT workshop were given proper identity cards and badges; when asked who we were, we were very straightforward: 'We are raising funds for the Unification Church.' We always had our cards ready for inspection.

But when we started selling the wooden roses, a member of the team arrived who had a different approach. Sophie was about twelve years older then me, and had been a member for a great deal longer.

Before she joined, she had been a member of a very strange sect. That was part of the 'things of old', and she rarely spoke about her past, but I gathered that she was married, that her husband had left her long ago, and that she had a twelve-year old daughter who lived with Sophie's parents.

Her job was to be 'team mother' for our team, which meant that she made sure that everything ran smoothly, and that Stephen and the rest of the team had everything we needed; she also went fundraising with us herself most of the time. It was understood that she had a pastoral role as well, but I found that hard to accept. She was a very intense person, apparently unable to make suggestions without seeming at the same time to regard you as incompetent. She seized on the arrival of the new roses as an opportunity to issue a general challenge to further efforts.

'You have a very saleable product there, Jacqui. How do you plan to sell it?'

I shrugged my shoulders. 'I've been making my goals. I'll just carry on the same way.'

'Maybe it's time to try something new. Tell me, Jacqui, if somebody approached you on the street selling something, and said they were a student trying to work their way through college, would you buy?'

'Of course I would,' I said. 'Wouldn't anybody?'

'OK then,' said Sophie briskly. 'Be a student working your way through college.'

It took a few moments for her meaning to sink in. 'But – that's not true, it's a lie,' I protested.

'It's more of – ah – a deception,' Sophie responded. 'What you could call a heavenly deception ... Do you think it's important that the product should be sold? Of course you do. It's important for the customers, it's important for Father. So what's more important – that we should do this work as well as we possibly can, make good goals, sell product – or that we should be content with going on as we have been doing?'

Put that way, I was forced to agree. I found it very hard to accept, especially as Sophie's manner was so overbearing. But when I tried it on the street I saw that it really was effective. After a while I no longer announced that I was a member of the Unification Church, nor that I was raising funds for its work. Instead I said that I was trying to raise money on my own account, to see me through to graduation. I found many sympathetic hearers, and I sold a lot of product.

In any case, after a short time we became a 'business team'; we told purchasers that we were in business for ourselves, and denied that we were part of any religious organisation. The lie came all the easier because Sophie had taught me how to hide the truth already.

The roses came in different sizes and colours, from small buds to full-blown blossoms. When a customer wanted to buy several in a vase I allowed them to choose the blooms and the colours they wanted, and then I would choose a nice vase. I had a steel-reinforced box that had once held bottles of Seven-Up, and I kept the vases in the front and the roses, in their packaging, at the back. In bad weather I stretched a sheet of polythene over it, and the whole thing made a very effective wayside stall.

I had all the equipment. Besides a bag to hold the money, I had a spray-bottle of glycerine mixed with rose oil to freshen up the flowers when I was on a sundrenched sidewalk or in a hot factory. Sometimes the customer wanted a particular bloom opened up or closed more than it was, and this could be done by misting with a little glycerine, but it was even more necessary when the flowers began to dry out – then they looked like blotting paper and tore as easily. Caring for the product was very important.

There were bad days even among the new successes. I had a particularly difficult time relating to Sophie, who seemed to have a special and unwelcomed interest in my spiritual well-being.

'Oh, Jacqui,' she often said, 'you ought to try to control your temper.' But she said it so intensely, looking into my eyes with a sweet and irritating sincerity, that however placid and tolerant I might have been before she said it, I was fuming after she had. She was constantly trying to make 'conditions' for me, to urge me into yet more self-denial and rigorous living, and I found it infuriating. Sophie rapidly became a major source of tension in my life.

But I was pulled through such difficulties on a tide of achievement. On the special holy days of the Church I began to receive photographs of the True Parents and their children, each photograph sent from the Church headquarters in New York and presented to me as a mark of achieving particularly high sales. These large glossy portraits I treasured. They were likenesses of the Messiah. Nor was I unique; all our team consistently achieved very high goals, and soon there were many glossy photographs tucked away in our personal belongings ... They were never left lying around, and were treated with great reverence; I propped one up by my head while I slept.

News of our success had clearly impressed New York, for after several months of successful rose-selling, Mr Fujama one day made an exciting announcement.

'We have been asked to go over to Canada and begin fundraising there,' he said.

A babble of interest arose. People wanted to know when – 'Almost immediately,' he said – and why: 'But there's a team already in Canada, Mr Fujama!'

'Wouldn't it be real wrong for us to fundraise on their patch?' asked Sophie. I reacted immediately against what I regarded as her soulful self-righteousness, but Mr Fujama, who was much better at handling her than I was (though she wasn't constantly criticising *him*, I reminded myself), answered her thoughtfully.

'It would usually be very wrong, Sophie, because it would take away from the Canadian team the rewards that are rightfully theirs. They have claimed Canada for God just as we have claimed Detroit.' He added, without a trace of humour, 'Unfortunately, they are not doing so well at all.' A shadow of genuine sorrow fell across his face. 'I think Father is grieved with the Canadian team. We must work very hard to make sure *we* do not grieve him.'

He pointed to a large map on the noticeboard that hung on the wall. 'We are to begin in Ontario, and we will work our way west. The team will be in Canada for several weeks at a time, and will come back to the centre here from time to time. Joel will be the captain of the new team. Sophie will be team mother.'

A look of sweet surprise passed over Sophie's face as she bowed her head in submission. I felt like throwing up. Did we have to take her with us to Canada? On the other hand, I liked Joel, who was an aggressive, dominating person I couldn't help responding to favourably, and Sarah, my ally and example, was also going to be on the team.

So began a period of fantastic success in fundraising. We began in Toronto, and there we rented a house. For over two months we systematically fundraised our way through Ontario, and then we came back to Detroit for a weekend. The following week we went back to Canada and continued our progress west. We worked the big cities in the same way – cities like Winnipeg, Calgary and Edmonton. We stayed in each area for three months, returning to Detroit between areas. We ended up in Vancouver, where we stayed for six months. Arriving there gave me a distinctly odd feeling; it was on my way to Barney Coombes's community in Vancouver that I had first met with the Unification Church. But we were so busy fundraising that I never had the chance to enquire where the community was, even had I still wanted to visit it.

Sophie was as much an irritation in Canada as she had been in Detroit, and I frequently found my nerves fraying as she nagged away at the weak points which I knew perfectly well I had. 'Oh, Jacqui, have you thought what a *good* condition it would make for Father's blessing, if you were just to stop biting your nails?'

'Yes, I *have*,' I retorted grimly, and stuffed my fingers with their chewed ends deep into my pocket. I knew that if I were more peaceable as a person I wouldn't have such problems in dealing with Sophie and would probably be able to laugh her moralising off.

Yet it was in Canada that I began to make colossal sums of money. When we were in Detroit to celebrate True Children's Day, Mr Fujama handed me a small package wrapped in tissue. He beamed. 'From Father,' he said. I opened it. Inside was a tiny gold medallion on a gold chain. Mr Fujama took it from me and placed it gently round my neck. 'This month, Jacqui,' he explained, 'you were among the top ten fund-raisers in America. Father is very pleased.'

Everybody clapped, and I stood a little awkwardly, unused to such praise; but inside, I was glowing with satisfaction.

'Thank you,' I managed to say, and fingered the medallion appreciatively. I'd seen them before, but had never thought that I would one day earn one for myself.

That night, Sophie drew me aside. 'I'm so glad,' she said.

'Thanks, Sophie.' I was still basking in pleasure, and Sophie's comment increased it.

'Though really,' she added, 'it's a very strong team. You mustn't be content to stay where you are. Everyone is level-pegging with you, you need to set yourself even higher goals, you know?'

'Of course I know,' I said defensively. It was as if a shadow had fallen across all the pleasure and satisfaction I was feeling. *Trust Sophie*! I thought savagely.

But I treasured my award and resolved to work even harder for Father.

14 WINNIPEG

Winnipeg: city (1971 est. pop. 246,246), provincial capital,
SE Man., Canada, at the confluence of the Red and
Assiniboine rivers. It is the largest city of the Prairie
Provinces and one of the world's largest wheat markets. A
railroad, commercial, industrial and distribution centre,
it has an international airport, railroad shops, grain
elevators, stockyards, meat-packing plants, flour mills,
and varied manufacturing industries. The city's history
reflects the history of early French and British explorers
and fur traders.

[*International Geographic Encyclopaedia and Atlas*,
Macmillan Press, 1979.]

'Joel,' I ventured, 'I don't feel very well.'

More months had gone by, and I had now been with the
Unification Church for almost two years. We were doing
well in Canada. Joel was a very good fundraiser himself, and
demanded very high standards from his team.

'What's the problem?' Joel was non-committal.

'It's these stomach aches I've been having. They're really
starting to bother me.'

Joel frowned. 'Stomach aches are often psychosomatic. I
don't believe you're really sick. You need to get out and
work harder.'

I was angry, but at the same time I responded very
positively to Joel's scepticism. He was an unpredictable
person, given to sweeping decisions and near-impossible

goals in which he set a lead so vigorously that there was little one could do but follow.

'All right, Joel,' I acquiesced meekly. 'I expect it will sort itself out.'

I had wondered whether the stomach pains might have be caused by nervous stress. I was going through a bad patch; for some reason I was finding it hard to make my goals, and Sophie, who was having a very successful few months, was not slow to point out my poor performance to me. Ordinarily I wouldn't have worried too much – the other people on my team were friends I'd worked with for a while, and I felt strongly supported by them. But when Sophie began to needle me, I allowed it to disturb me more than I ought to have done. My resistance was lowered because I really wasn't feeling very well. There was a recurring slight nausea and abdominal pain which was never serious enough to go to a doctor with, but which, over a period of months, was beginning to have a very tiring effect on me.

Not long afterwards, my frustration with Sophie flared up at last, one morning in Winnipeg when she and I were fundraising together.

That day I was on edge during morning service, and, hunched against the swaying of the van, I began to chew my fingernails. Immediately, I felt an elbow nudging me in the ribs. When I looked round I saw Sophie shaking her head at me. I groaned inwardly and clenched my fists.

Afterwards Sophie worried away at the subject.

'I guess you really ought to make it a special condition, Jacqui. You could offer it up to our Heavenly Father as a sacrifice.'

I didn't respond, but a black cloud was settling on my spirits. Sophie continued relentlessly.

'I realise you'd prefer not to, but isn't that the whole point? I mean surely it should cost, that's what a condition is. Think about it, why don't you?'

I stared at the road bleakly. Ancient Winnipeg landmarks

glided into view and disappeared behind us, but I took no notice. This was in itself a sign of my inner turmoil. I loved Canada and always enjoyed the scenery, even if I was travelling a road I'd travelled many times already.

'Well, here we are, anyway, Jacqui.' The car pulled up. We had reached my drop-off point. Joel, who was due later that day to fly to Detroit for the weekend, waved me off. 'See you when I get back.' As I got out of the car, Sophie swivelled round and looked fixedly into my eyes. 'Think about it, Jacqui.'

I picked up my flowers and walked off without a word, which depressed me even more because I knew I would have to apologise to her later.

An hour later I had made twenty dollars, and most of the people I'd approached had been put off by my gloomy manner. Hardly anybody was around in the area I was working in. The prospect of spending the next few hours flogging myself into action to secure enough sales to make my goal was not pleasant.

'After all,' I announced to nobody in particular, 'it all has to be done again anyway. It doesn't matter how much I make today, tomorrow I have to start from nothing and make the whole amount all over again. It isn't *fair*!'

The weight of the task seemed overwhelming. I was supposedly out there to pay indemnity for my past sins. When they were paid for I would have to start paying for my ancestors' sins. The people who bought my roses were in part paying for their sins by so doing, though they did not realise it. It was as if I were bound to an enormous wheel, endlessly rotating throughout history, which I had to keep turning by my own efforts.

I tried to shake myself out of the despair that was growing inside me. *Don't let Sophie deflect you*, I told myself grimly. *You are working to bring about the kingdom of God on earth. That's what's important.* But try as I might, I could not stop the depression from growing.

Suddenly I made a decision. The railway station was not far away. It was warm and I could sit down there. Like a sleepwalker, I turned away from my area and walked to the station.

I used some of the morning's takings to store my product in a left-luggage locker. Slipping the key into my pocket, I decided to become an ordinary citizen for a few hours. I wandered round the station, looking at the things in the kiosks, and finally slumped down on a bench, staring up at the high vaulting of the roof.

People came and went; some sat near me and looked incuriously at the brooding figure hunched on the bench staring into space. After a while I began to feel hungry. I had some money which had been given me for food, so I sat in a coffee bar on the station forecourt and had some sandwiches and coffee.

I sat in the coffee bar for a long time, until it began to be crowded and other people wanted my seat. Inside my head, all my thoughts were revolving, round and round. I was barely conscious of time passing.

I decided to wander round the city, and walked along streets I'd never seen before, until I had no idea where I was. Eventually I found a public library, and gratefully sat at a table, propped a book up in front of me, and was fast asleep within minutes.

I woke up with a start. There was hardly anybody in the library. The clock above the entrance showed eight-thirty. The library was about to close.

Back on the street I panicked. I had no idea where I was, but I knew that I had missed the pick-up. People would be looking for me. Joel would have left for home by now. If I didn't come back, it would be Sophie who would have to ring Detroit and tell the Fujamas I was missing. I had no idea what to do.

Eventually, after asking several people for directions, I

made my way back to the railway station and sat there for an hour. This time the station was almost deserted, and I was receiving some very odd glances from the officials. The high ceiling was lost in shadows, and long periods of quiet were punctuated by the coming and going of trains. It was an eerie place at night, and I was becoming quite nervous.

There were not many options open to me. I could sleep in the station; I could walk the streets all night; or I could go back to the hotel and take whatever punishment was waiting for me there. The decision didn't take much thought. I was sick of the station after spending most of the day there, and I had an uncomfortable feeling that one or two of the staff were considering calling the police. I decided to walk back to the hotel.

My drop-off point had been about three miles from the hotel. The roads were reasonably lit, and there was not much traffic. It was mid-summer, but the night air was chill. I hadn't eaten since lunchtime, and I was hungry. The gnawing ache in my abdomen began to bother me again. I began walking.

There was a man on the opposite sidewalk, keeping pace with me, stopping when I stopped and speeding up when I attempted to lose him. I stole a look at him. He was young, and wore trendy clothes. He saw me looking at him.

'Hey, where you goin'?' he called to me. I ignored the question and strode resolutely on.

'Wait, woman, can't you slow down? Maybe we can walk together. Where *are* you goin'?'

When I said nothing, he crossed the street and took up a position a few yards behind me, keeping step with me and remaining at the same distance. His whining, heavily accented voice continued to probe.

'What's a pretty girl like you doin' out alone, anyway? You need lookin' after. I tell you, if I had a pretty young woman like you I sure wouldn't let her out on her own – no sir.'

I was too scared to turn round. However fast I walked he stayed at the same distance behind me. Stories I'd heard of muggings and rapes came to my mind. The crisp footsteps of the man behind me tapped out a measured sound of walking, and I subconsciously braced myself for the sudden rush and attack from behind which I was sure was going to happen.

'Can't you speak, woman? You deaf or somethin'?'

Suddenly I heard a car coasting down the street behind me, and then the squeal of brakes. I turned involuntarily. A police patrol car was pulled up on the kerbside. The man had disappeared.

A policeman wound down a window and called to me. 'Was he giving you trouble?'

I went back to the car. I was trembling from delayed reaction. 'Yes, he was. Thank you for stopping.'

'Do you have your ID?'

I was nonplussed. My visa had long since expired. 'Uh – it's back home.'

The officer stared at me hard. 'And what are you doing on the streets this time of night? Are you asking for trouble?'

'I got stranded,' I said. 'I'm walking back to my hotel.' I gave them the name of the hotel and looked longingly at the police car. 'Ah – do you think ...'

'Ma'am, we don't go anywhere near your hotel. Walk fast, stay in the streetlights, and don't get talking to people. You don't have far to go.'

I began to walk on. As the police driver started up his engine, the officer shouted, 'And another thing. Just don't do such a tomfool stupid thing *ever* again, you hear that?'

About half a mile further on, another man stepped out of the shadows.

'Got the time?'

'It's after midnight,' I muttered. He stood in front of me, blocking my way. He was middle-aged, good looking in a coarse way. 'I know a bar that's open,' he said in a slurred voice. 'Wanna come with me?'

'No thank you,' I replied. 'Let me past, please.'

We stood facing each other in a pool of lamplight and I was very frightened. 'You wanna dance?' he demanded. 'Roun' the corner there's a club where we could dance.'

'Please, let me go,' I pleaded. His eyes narrowed.

'You wanna have some real fun? I gotta place roun' here, we could go to my place. No problem.'

I broke into a run, which was probably the most dangerous thing I could have done, but fortunately the man was drunker than I realised and made no attempt to follow. Soon I was clear, in a broad well-lit highway about three-quarters of a mile from the hotel.

I was in a state of confusion. I knew that I was disobeying every rule of the Church, and that I was now openly rebelling against the instructions we had been given. I knew that I had set up a 'bad condition' and that I was open to attacks from demons. As I thought about it I could sense real powers of evil lining the road, reaching out for me as I passed. I broke into a fast trot and did not stop again until I arrived at the hotel.

I arrived panting at the main entrance. I could see the van parked outside. So the team was back. In our suite they would be preparing for bed. Probably they were worried at my disappearance.

The thought of Joel's sharp tongue, and what he would do about my misbehaviour during the day, made me deeply apprehensive. But it was imagining what Sophie would say that finally stopped me from going in. I just didn't have the nerve to go up and face them all. 'I've really done it this time,' I thought.

Instead, I crossed the road to a motel and lay down on the doorstep of one of the chalets. I dozed fitfully all night, and woke stiff and slightly nauseous as the first light of dawn was breaking. Then, afraid of being reported for loitering, I hid

within sight of the hotel entrance and waited for the team to
leave for the day.

We always left the key in the hotel office when we were
going out, so it was a simple matter for me to collect it. Once
in our suite I found some money of my own, which I had
won as a fundraising prize. I put on some warm clothing,
and went out again.

I was ravenously hungry. Though I knew that spending
money on food was not a good thing unless the money had
been blessed and put aside for that purpose, I went for lunch
to a really big restaurant in the city and bought an enormous
meal. I had chilli, and even ordered a dessert. Feelings of
guilt were competing with my craving for food, and my
appetite won. I felt afraid and insecure. For the past two
years all my life had been spent in well-defined roles with
well-defined functions. Now I had broken all that, in a
situation over which I had long since lost control. I felt
extremely vulnerable.

Afterwards I went back to the library, and sitting
half asleep at one of the tables the enormity of my escapade
really began to hit me. The feast I had bought was
what finally brought it home to me. I was wracked with
guilt.

And yet I couldn't face Sophie. I was stuck in an impasse. I
had nowhere to go except the Unification Church, but I had
broken its rules and trampled on its regulations. In the end, I
rang Detroit. I reversed the charges and asked to speak to
Mrs Fujama. She had heard of my disappearance and was
very worried. As she spoke to me on the telephone she was
crying.

'We were so worried about you – come back, it doesn't
matter what you have done, we still love you and we've
missed you.'

I wept, Mrs Fujama wept, and I told her the whole story,
about Sophie, about my sense of failure. 'I'll talk to them
about it,' she promised. And so I went back to the hotel.

As it happened, Joel had been called to New York the previous day, straight after he had dropped us in the morning, so he hadn't known anything about my disappearance. I was overwhelmed by my reception: there was no criticism, just happiness that I was back. In the next few days I was able to talk to Sophie with an openness that had never been possible before, and she seemed genuinely shaken by the fact that my disappearance had been provoked by her treatment of me. We reached a kind of understanding, and things were certainly better, but our working together was always somewhat precarious, and we were often tense with each other.

A similar process was happening with my parents. Things were much easier, and our letters were less full of recriminations and hostility. They sent news of mutual friends, and I sent long letters home full of the places I'd been to and the people I'd met. When they invited me to go back home for a holiday, I sensed that it was not a ploy to recapture me but a genuine desire to see me again.

I mentioned the request to Mr and Mrs Fujama, but was not surprised at their reaction. 'God wants you here, Jacqui. There is so much to do. And besides, would you be able to get back into America?'

It was an important point. My visa had long since expired. I was technically an illegal immigrant. I had told my parents that I had renewed my visa; but in fact it was very unlikely that I would have been able to secure an extension had I applied for one. So I had never bothered.

I wrote to my parents, explaining that it was impossible to leave the work at present.

And still our fundraising successes continued. We became the most successful team in the country; at our height we were making up to $12,000 a month each before expenses were deducted. We were consistently making $700 a day on average, and on one memorable day, selling wooden roses, I made $1,700. My personal monthly best was $35,000.

The awards from the New York headquarters of the Church, which Mr and Mrs Fujama presented on 'holy days' to those of us who had been conspicuously successful, became increasingly splendid.

Before long I had five small gold medallions, and added to them five much larger ones which were made of solid gold and were worth, I estimated, about £100 each for their gold content. They were for being in the top three fundraisers.

I was also presented with a number of small ornamental 'pins', which were for less sensational achievements. I had several white ones, which were awarded for making an average $300–$350 gross per day for three months in a row (including Sundays). At the time, it worked out at about $250 a day after expenses had been paid.

I also had some pink pins, which represented $6,000, and a large number of green ones which were given for making $4,000.

They in fact represented a very large amount of money, because all the qualifying sums were net; a white pin probably meant that you had really made $10,000 gross.

The 'pins' (which were actually tiny medallions) all had a common design. Two hills, one larger than the other, were outlined in gold and filled in with the appropriate colour. Round the outside they bore the four radiating arrows of the Unification Church symbol. The summits of the two hills formed a letter 'M', which, we were told, was M for Moon and M for money, and also symbolised going through valleys.

The pins were given to us by our leaders, and Sophie, seeing me presented with yet another, would usually take the opportunity to lecture me. She was perpetually urging me to put sterner and sterner conditions upon myself. All the rest of the team also received pins, but I never noticed Sophie being critical of them.

On one occasion our team was the top team in America and we were all given Walkman tape players, and we wore them everywhere we went and listened to them as we travelled between areas. Sometimes at night, too tired to sleep, I finally drifted into dreamland listening to the soothing sounds of my prize.

My most treasured trophy of all was a photograph of Reverend Moon himself, in a beautiful polished wood frame. It was presented to me by Mr Fujama, and I was the only person who got one. It was given to me to mark one memorable month in which I became top fundraiser in America.

Meanwhile, the pains in my stomach were not going away. I was developing an obsessive interest in my state of health, and with some reason. The aches had become cramps, with my abdominal muscles knotted into hard boards – if somebody had kicked me in the midriff it wouldn't have hurt me.

But our success as a team continued; the prizes we gained became more splendid. I sometimes looked at the bag of jewellery I had been given, and reflected wryly that I had given up all my possessions to join the Church, and now my only possessions were a collection of expensive ornaments.

Much of the success of our team was directly due to Joel's leadership. I had never met anybody quite like him. He was different from everybody else on the team, and his behaviour was often unpredictable. I never quite knew how he was going to treat me. Once, when I didn't make my goal, he threw a plateful of food at me; and when I was reluctant to work, he would shout at me at the top of his voice, galvanising me into action. Often he would punch me, and I was always unsure whether it was meant as a punishment or an encouragement.

Most of the team leaders were somewhat aloof and reserved, but Joel was boisterous and hearty. He was the life and soul of the few social occasions we had. To Joel, fundraising was the most important thing in life, and everything else had to take a back seat.

So when I went to Joel and told him that my pains were getting worse, I didn't have very high hopes of sympathy. I was not proved wrong.

'I just feel sick,' I protested one day, sitting in the van as we were about to leave for our area. 'How can I have a right attitude when I'm feeling like this? I really think I ought to stay behind today. Perhaps I need a day's rest.'

Joel snorted. 'Well, why don't you just *be* sick?'

'I can't,' I said miserably. 'It's not that kind of feeling sick.'

He grabbed me by the elbow and hustled me out of the van. We stood by the kerb. 'All right,' said Joel, 'stick your fingers down your throat!'

'Wha-at?' I exclaimed weakly.

'Stick your fingers down your throat. *Make* yourself sick. Then we can get on with what we're supposed to be doing.' And he stood over me as I did what I was told. Then, after I had vomited into the kerb and was pale-faced and shivering from reaction, he bundled me back into the van.

'Right. Now you can go out and make $500.' He beamed aggressively. 'And I want you to run all the way.'

I hated him for that. I did what I was told, but inside I was boiling with anger. I made $500 that day.

Resentment against the leaders was often a sign that I was having a particularly bad time spiritually. Most of the time I found Joel's vigorous leadership stimulating and challenging, but sometimes, if I was having one of my bad days, I would brood over the way he treated me, and would tell myself bitterly, '*I'd* be on top of things if I had a life like his – driving around in the van all day, just dropping people off and buying the food and doing the administration and phoning the leaders …'

Such bitterness and resentment was capable of rooting itself very deeply inside me, and I found that once I had given in to it, it was very difficult to shake off. Bad days became bad weeks as I succumbed more and more to my bitterness and selfishness. When that happened, I felt real guilt, and it was as if Satan was pointing a finger at me in accusation.

The only way out of it was to throw myself into energetic acts of obedience; when I was fasting, or 'setting a condition', it was difficult to be absorbed in my own problems. So by hard work and discipline, I pulled myself out of the depression and got back to the business of wholehearted fundraising.

An unexpected source of encouragement at these times was my correspondence with my parents. Our letters had become much less strained, and I enjoyed receiving them now. I felt I could trust Mum and Dad not to put pressure on me to leave the Church.

I was right in that belief, though I did not know it. They had already turned down offers from a national newspaper to run a campaign to highlight my case, and had also – with some reluctance – decided not to pay a professional 'deprogrammer' to kidnap me and force me to renounce Reverend Moon.

They had entrusted my future to God, they were sure that he would bring me home at the right time, and they were content to wait.

15 JOEL

Every one of us must realise what Jesus should have done. Jesus should have gotten married sinlessly. Jesus came to marry a sinless spouse and to have sinless children – to realise sinless family. Christians never knew it. But now that we know, we ourselves, everyone of us, must get married sinlessly and must have sinless children and must establish a sinless family centering on ourselves. Otherwise, Jesus' mission can't be fulfilled. We must be the Messiah for our own family.

[Ken Sudo, *120 Day Training Program*, Unification Church training document, New York, n.d.]

The stomach pains became so severe that I lost my will to work almost entirely, and even Joel began to realise that something was really wrong. In fact he became quite considerate, though he still tried to motivate me in the only way he knew – by shouting at me. But in times of recreation, or relaxing on the way home after a hard day, he would sometimes slip an arm around my shoulder and hug me. Sometimes he pummelled me in mock fights, though not the semi-violent punches that he had previously given me to try to get me out to work.

I was glad that Joel had changed; it was one less thing to worry about. And a useful by-product of this change of heart was that he took my illness seriously and asked the Fujamas to look into it.

The next time we returned to Detroit they asked me for all the details.

'How long has it been going on?'

'Oh, for a long time. The pains started really quietly. I hardly noticed them at first. Now they're really noticeable.'

Mrs Fujama was very concerned. 'We must have this seen to,' she said. 'We'll arrange for you to be seen by a doctor. You must not go back to Canada until you have been properly examined.' She gave me a penetrating glance. 'Have you been worrying about anything? Are your problems with Sophie still upsetting you?'

'I'm just tired,' I said. 'Feeling unwell has really taken it out of me. Sometimes I can hardly drag myself out of doors in the mornings.'

'Many of us go through times like that,' Mr Fujama said gently. 'Satan desires to have you, he will fight to have you, and this is one of his ways.'

'That's what Joel said,' I acknowledged. 'And I've tried – oh, I've tried so hard – but I'm so tired and I feel so *sick* all the time.'

'Is there anything you would like us to do? Is there any way we can help?'

I thought for a moment. 'I'd like to go on a workshop. You know, you told me at the beginning, when we're on MFT we can go to a seven-day workshop in New York. I'd really like to go. I think I need to take time out, to get my bearings spiritually – and I think that's what going to a workshop would do for me.' My voice was wobbling and rising in pitch. I feared I was going to cry. 'I want to go. I really do. Can I?'

Mrs Fujama nodded gravely. 'We'll see.'

Mr Fujama put a hand on my shoulder. 'These decisions are not made just by one or two,' he said. 'Father knows best. We must just wait and see.'

The doctor I went to see was a very kind Indian lady who

took the trouble to talk to her patients. She believed in putting them in the picture, and she showed me charts and diagrams to illustrate the various things she was saying.

'You see, Miss Williams,' she explained in a friendly, matter-of-fact way, 'pains in the stomach are very difficult to diagnose. All your major organs are in the abdomen or near by. Often the origin of such pains is in the mind.'

I nodded. So Joel had had a point.

'Tell me, what sort of life do you lead? You work for a religious community, isn't that right?'

'Yes, I do.' I began to tell her about my working day. She listened intently, her head on one side, her face betraying little reaction to the things I was telling her.

'So you begin work at 7 a.m.,' she repeated, writing notes in careful biro on her pad. 'So that would be – how many hours sleep?'

'Four,' I said. Then, hastily, 'but on Sunday mornings we sleep late.'

'I see.' The pen moved purposefully across the paper. 'Now, what do you normally eat for breakfast?'

I told her everything. I told her about the hamburgers, the fast-food lunches snatched between areas, the late-night fried chicken and the coffee gulped in the van. I explained that I was eating a very fatty diet, mainly comprising convenience foods. I told her about fasting, and how Joel and I had often made a 'condition' where we would not eat anything until we'd made $500, and so we would often work without food right through from waking to ten or eleven at night. And I told her how on cold days, when the temperature was 50° below freezing, I would run all day from street to street, and flop down, sweating and exhausted, in the van.

'And did it occur to anybody that your trouble might be due to this very unusual lifestyle?'

'They thought it was stress. I was told it might be psychosomatic. Do you think it might be?'

She grunted non-committally, sat back and studied her notes. 'Please remove your outer garments. I want to examine you.'

Afterwards, as I dressed, the doctor delivered her verdict. 'I can't find anything organically wrong with you,' she stated. 'I have checked you out and everything is reasonably normal. You're run down, and you should lose some weight. You're eating all the wrong things. But as for your pains, I can't tell you what is causing them.'

She took a pad of forms and scribbled down some details. Tearing the sheet off, she handed it to me. 'I want you to see a gynaecologist,' she said. 'There is a possibility that that might solve the problem.'

The gynaecologist cross-examined me, gave me a blood test and various other tests, put me on the Pill (to regularise my menstrual cycle), and told me to come back in a few weeks. I visited her several times, but neither she nor the Indian doctor could find anything specifically wrong.

When I rejoined the team Joel was unusually considerate and kind. I assumed that the Fujamas had telephoned him and told him to give me an easy time.

I had a nasty shock, however, when a girl on the team called Bobbie, whom I didn't know particularly well, took me to one side and spoke to me frankly.

'I think you ought to watch out with Joel, Jacqui.'

'What on earth do you mean?' I had no idea what she was talking about.

'I think he's very, very fond of you – in a way that he shouldn't be.'

I laughed outright. 'But he's matched, he's going to be Blessed; he's going to be married – he's not interested in me!'

Bobbie pursed her lips. 'I think you should really take care,' she said. 'Maybe you should talk to somebody about it. One of the leaders.'

I remembered the long talks with Kristy in San Francisco

about romantic involvement in the Unification Church, and what she had said about the disciplining of those who transgressed the practice of the community. 'That could be really harmful to Joel, to talk like that,' I countered. 'Why, he might have to leave the team.'

Bobbie smiled thinly. 'That's what I mean,' she said.

It was nearly New Year, and we had been promised the weekend off. Over the holiday we went to stay at a palatial hotel in Kalamazoo, a city in the farming region to the west of Detroit near to Lake Michigan. It was wonderful; we stayed there for three days and did no work at all. We even slept in beds, which was incredibly luxurious after sleeping on the floor in sleeping bags. The food was superb – a far cry from hamburgers and French fries.

We went skiing, skated, and thoroughly enjoyed ourselves in the crisp wintry sunshine. But I became very worried by Joel's attitude to me, especially in view of what Bobbie had said earlier. He seemed to be making every possible opportunity to be with me. He didn't make passes, nothing that he said was objectionable, and I was fairly certain that nobody else could see what was happening; but he was definitely taking a special interest in me, and I felt very uncomfortable indeed.

So, at the end of the holiday, with Bobbie's warning fresh in my mind, I asked Mrs Fujama if I could talk to her.

'It's Joel,' I said awkwardly. 'I think he's being just too friendly. And I'm specially worried because he is already matched.'

Mrs Fujama sighed. 'All right, Jacqui. Thank you for telling me. We will see to it.'

I learned afterwards that there had followed a really dreadful confrontation. Joel was summoned to appear before the Fujamas, and apparently he confessed that he had been growing fond of me. He was with the Fujamas for several hours. The next day, he left. We didn't say goodbye.

I only pieced the story together from odd comments, so I

never really heard the whole of it, but obviously Bobbie had been right. I was sorry to see Joel go. I had liked him a lot, despite his overbearing and forceful personality.

He was replaced by Jim, who was also a very good fundraiser. Under his leadership the team continued to do well. But before long he was transferred to take charge of a team that was doing very badly.

Our next team leader was Matthew. At the same time as his arrival, some people left our team and were sent to other work, and the team as I had known it, which had remained as a unit the whole time that Joel had been leader, began to split up and change.

A further major change was that we were taken out of Canada. I heard that the Canadian teams had complained that we were making too much money and spoiling things for them; and they had apparently requested that we be stopped from going over the border. So we wound down our Canadian operations and once again worked from and around Detroit, going away from the Detroit centre for about a month at a time.

I was very frustrated with Matthew. He didn't inspire me at all; he had no personal charisma, and was hesitant to take a leading role. Worse, when I told him I was unwell he didn't argue. 'Oh – stay in the back of the van,' he said. Part of me was grateful and part of me felt terribly guilty. I had a very real sense of loss for those days in Canada, and a lot of my 'fighting spirit' (a term we often used to encapsulate the sense of burning purpose we were encouraged to have constantly at the forefront of our minds) was evaporating under Matthew's leadership. He never pushed me in any way. And that was bad, because it wasn't just the outside world we were supposed to be battling against; it was our own laziness and selfishness.

He was under orders to give me easy duties because of my health, and I was limited to eight hours' fundraising per day. I was able to stop carrying heavy packages of product;

previously, I had manhandled heavy loads without thinking twice about it. It was a blessing, because some of the dreadful tiredness began to lift. But I felt a fraud; I was afraid that I had exaggerated my stomach pains, and I was soon burdened with a sense of guilt. I knew the importance of fundraising. Was I opting out of God's work just to give myself an easy time?

After all, being ill – dominated by the demands of the body – was in a sense a victory of Cain, I reflected. All the sympathy was simply creating the illusion that illness was acceptable. *Joel wouldn't have let me lie here*, I told myself often. *He'd bawl me out and push me on to the streets*.

Though I was only working eight hours I still had to make a goal. I was transferred to the team that was making the lowest results, and my guilt was relieved a little by the fact that in my eight hours I was making more than most of the rest of the team made in sixteen.

It was during this period of frustration that I received a letter from England from my parents.

'We understand you can't leave America,' wrote Mum, 'so we are coming to visit you! We plan to stay a week or so and want you to take some time to have a short holiday with us.'

Rather to my surprise, the Fujamas agreed.

'It will be good to have your parents meet our Brothers and Sisters,' said Mrs Fujama. 'You can show them some of America and perhaps they will understand more of the work you are doing for Father with us. Yes, write to them and say they will be welcome.' Perhaps they saw my state of mind and thought that a holiday would restore my health and enthusiasm.

We had a wonderful time. It wasn't a confrontation. We carefully avoided the most controversial subjects, and talked mostly about America and home. As my parents were now attending my old church, there was lots of news to catch up on.

Our reunion was a happy one, and I think they enjoyed meeting the Fujamas and the team when we entertained my parents at the flat. But for most of the time we were travelling, sightseeing. We went to Niagara Falls, and then made for Buffalo on the Canadian border, planning to go into Canada and back down to Detroit.

The problem, of course, was my passport. It was easy enough to get in and out of Canada if you were prepared to say you were an American, as I had been doing successfully for months, but it was a very different matter to go through the official immigration procedures.

'I've got a problem, Dad,' I said, as we approached the border post. 'I can't go through as an English person, I haven't got my passport with me. But don't worry, I'll pretend to be American. Americans are excused the formalities.'

Dad exploded in fury. 'You're not going to tell lies. You can tell them the truth. Tell them you're English and you haven't got your passport. You can always send it later.'

'It's not worth the hassle, it really isn't.'

Dad was adamant. I stood my ground. 'Either we go through like that or we don't go through at all, Dad. I'm *sorry*.' There was an edge to my voice. Mum and Dad were both angry, and were losing their tempers.

'How can you do this? You're supposed to be a Christian,' stormed Dad. 'How can you be so dishonest and claim to be a missionary? You're not even a Christian if you can do a wicked thing like that!'

I tried to argue back, but Dad was too angry.

'All I can say is that this group you've got yourself tied up with certainly isn't a Christian church, not if that's how they've taught you to behave.' All the carefully avoided controversies were suddenly brought into prominence.

'I don't like it any more than you do,' I retorted. 'Do you think I want to break the law? But sometimes we have to.' I tried to justify myself. In the end I broke free and

marched through the Customs post, saying that I was
American and adopting a particularly convincing American
accent.

My father watched in anger, and then followed me into
the Customs post. Grabbing my arm, he pulled me back.

'Look,' he said to the officials. 'I'm English, and this is my
daughter. She's just told you she is American. She's not.
She's English. So what are you going to do about it?'

I was promptly taken back into the office and held there
for a long time while my parents waited outside. They were
both upset and angry, but I had settled into a cold, outraged
calm.

The officials had to send for an Immigration officer from
Buffalo. He was a tall, businesslike man.

'What's your name and situation?'

I said, 'I don't have my passport with me.'

'How long have you been in America?'

'A couple of years.'

'Do you have a green card?' he asked.

'I don't know,' I ventured. 'I don't carry my passport with
me.' I was bluffing for all I was worth.

He picked up the telephone and dialled his headquarters. I
could tell from the lengthy telephone conversation and the
questions he asked me that things were not looking good.
Eventually he replaced the receiver.

'Well, our information is that your visa is no longer
extended to you.' He took a blank form from his case and
began to fill it out in large, deliberate block capitals. 'And so
I therefore serve you with this form.'

It said that I had thirty days in which to leave the country.

They were quite nice to me, and obviously it wasn't a case
of smuggling. I gave the impression that I had forgotten my
passport and hadn't realised we would be going into Canada,
and we parted on good terms.

Outside, Dad and Mum were waiting.

'What happened?'

'Oh,' I said airily, 'it's fine – I just told them the situation …'

Dad was so furious – he had expected them to deport me back to England – that he went into the office to demand why they had been so lenient. Of course they told him what had really been on the form. When Dad emerged, furious because I had told him and Mum in my letters that my passport was in order, I made light of it. 'It just means I've got thirty days to get my visa renewed,' I said.

Mum could see that the argument was undoing much of the understanding that had built up between the three of us in the past few days, and she soothed him down. We resumed our journey. Of course we could not now go through Canada, so we went to Pittsburgh and Cleveland, and back to Detroit that way.

When they left, things had been patched up to some extent and we went to the airport together. Mum and I were crying. We all said goodbye and hugged one another, and I waved them off to their departure gate.

Later I wrote to them and said that I had been able to renew my visa. It was untrue. In fact I simply ignored the situation. It is fairly easy to hide in America if you are white and keep out of trouble. For a few months afterwards I changed my name as a precaution, and called myself Elizabeth Armstrong. I chose the surname because it was a wrestling match that had brought me into MFT in the first place.

16 QUESTIONS

In the Unification Church, many have joined and many
have left and few remain. We have lost many, many
brothers and sisters. They believed Father was the
Messiah; they received the Divine Principle. They made
deep determination to sacrifice their entire lives, yet many
left because we couldn't raise these members enough. We
must be a good leader ... it is a very simple truth.

[Ken Sudo, *120 Day Training Program*, New York, n.d.]

The hotel window was closed. Far below at street level was
the drone of traffic. In the next room two Sisters were
preparing food. I was lying in my sleeping bag, half asleep.
Somewhere on the streets my team was raising funds.

Perhaps because of the constant dull ache in my middle,
perhaps because of the side-effects of the Pill, I was
becoming weepy and depressed. In my depression my mind
fixed on the letter I'd had from Linda, my 'spiritual mother'
in England, begging me to come home. I remembered
getting her letter in Houston, and throwing it away; and I
remembered Linda herself. Her face came into my mind
sharply, in a way that I had remembered nobody from
England for two years apart from my parents.

Once I had begun to think of Linda, other people came
back to my mind; people from my old church, all the people
I'd known and loved there. And I thought back to the early
days in San Francisco when I had absorbed the Divine

Principle on the side of a sunlit hill, surrounded by people who really loved me.

I began to weep. *I'm thrown aside now*, I told myself bitterly. *Just because I can't earn money. I'm a problem member, a difficult case, because I'm not performing up to standard.*

I needed people whom I knew loved me. My emotions were raw and exposed; the strains of the previous months were having their effect.

I have always found it difficult to lose people. Lying on the floor in the hotel room I thought back to the people in the Unification Church who had meant such a great deal to me; Sam, Gregory, Joel and many others. Once they had gone they were gone for good.

No letter I had written to them had ever been answered. We weren't allowed to phone them. It would have been pointless anyway; they were all on different missions, and there was no central register of where a particular person was at a particular time. Orders arrived from New York, and often you didn't even know who was giving them; but you obeyed.

As I reflected on this my hurt increased. I began to wonder whether anybody had the same problem, or whether it was simply me.

I allowed myself to wallow in misery until the others came back. But I cheered myself up a little by reflecting that the next Blessing was not far away, when couples would be matched for later marriage. I would be eligible for matching by then. If I was matched to somebody then I would have the basis of an ongoing relationship, even if we were separated. We would be able to correspond, and to meet regularly – which was something that was not possible with any of the people I had lost contact with over the past two years.

In the meantime I was bowed down by disillusionment. The love that I had experienced in the early days did not seem to survive partings.

I came out of the depression, and told myself that it was because I was ill. I had not had time on my own for so long; this was the first 'free time' I had had of any significance for months. Even then, it wasn't really free time – I was supposed to be ill. So I slept, and watched TV, but I was not a free agent in the sense I had been before. It was all too easy to brood in such circumstances.

My frustration was largely contained; I had occasional bad days, but I might have several weeks of good days between them.

But when the bad days came, they came increasingly badly. I found myself spending one whole morning, for example, reflecting bleakly that it didn't matter how holy and righteous I was on one particular day, and made my goals, the next day I would have to start all over and do the same thing again.

Another time I was walking along a road in my area, thinking to myself, 'Shall I pray – or shan't I?' And as I wondered that, I realised I was caught in a double trap. Did I really believe it, I wondered; that if I didn't pray and make a spiritual effort, I wouldn't make my goal, and if I did do those things, I would? But some days I didn't pray, and I didn't make an effort, and I had the worst possible attitude and all sorts of wrong thoughts were going through my mind – and yet I made my goal and much more! And other days, I prayed and I worked and I had all the right attitudes, and I made hardly any money at all.

The formula isn't 100 per cent proof, I realised. And once the realisation had come, it never quite went away. I had lived my fundraising life as if I were on a treadmill. Once I became ill and started slowing down, I was in danger of falling off.

I had no doubts about Reverend Moon. I had never met him, but I knew his writings, and I was convinced he was the Messiah. But I was beginning to develop a barely discernible scepticism about aspects of the Church, and that in itself was worrying, because we were taught that we were all involved in the process of becoming perfect. Perfection seemed a long way away at times.

Nor did I contemplate leaving the Church. It wasn't a real option. Because I believed that Reverend Moon was the Messiah, there was nowhere to go outside the Church. Who could save mankind, if not the Messiah?

In any case, we were told that terrible things would happen if we left the Church. We were told that we would no longer be under God's protection, that there would be terrible consequences for our families. I had even been told that I would develop cancer if I left.

During my illness I thought through several areas of difficulty I had been aware of but had never had the time to analyse. For example, I had been told that nobody was ever on MFT for more than three years; yet I had been on MFT for three years now and no mention had been made of my moving on. Sophie, too, had been fundraising for seven years. Was I to be doing the same?

And when I did move, where would it be to? All the decisions that had been taken for me in the past had been conveyed by messages from New York. I seriously doubted that anyone there knew anything about me or what my needs and gifts were. I wished desperately that there was just one person, be it in New York or Korea, who knew my name and what I looked like, and who really cared for me. But all the time, it was as if I was a number on a list, and the kindness of the Fujamas and the relationships I was developing with my team members were liable to be overruled at any moment by the faceless, uncaring administrators in New York.

At the heart of my frustration was the loss of what had seemed to me to be an idyll, the California community. And I had heard that a number of people had been moved from

San Francisco to New York, because the leadership was aware that the California family was something very special, and they wanted to see if the same spirit could be developed in New York. There was a widespread sense of failure in the Church at that time. The home churches and witnessing centres, like the one I had been in in Detroit, were simply not working, and very few people were becoming members.

It occurred to me that possibly Ruthie and Sam and Jessica and other friends from California were in the New York family now. And that made me even more anxious to go on the seven-day New York workshop, about which I had asked Mr and Mrs Fujama.

Other people in the centre had been on the workshop, but Mr and Mrs Fujama seemed to be putting off sending me. 'Please can I go to New York?' I pleaded, but they were reluctant to commit themselves. 'First we must get you well,' they said.

Eventually, though the doctors never succeeded in diagnosing my illness, I was well enough to go back to a full working day, though I was still feeling very fragile. Being a full working member again was a great encouragement to me. I threw myself back into fundraising, and was soon making respectable goals again.

It was like emerging from a dark tunnel. It was simply not possible to dwell for long on doubts and resentments when working full-time, because the work was so demanding. And yet there was a kind of after-effect of my illness; a permanent weariness, and an underlying tinge of unhappiness.

From that point on, a process of questioning began, beginning with a questioning of myself. More and more doubts about my own ability to work off the indemnity of my own sins crowded in on me. I scrutinised my attitudes and was often unhappy at what I saw. I had often 'made a condition' that I would not eat until I made $500. But then, I recalled, I worked as hard as I could just so that I would make the money sooner and be able to eat.

Yet when I was in England I had been taught that as a Christian I ought not to do things for God solely because of personal profit I might receive from them. That made sense. So was the condition I had made of any value at all? On such days – and they were not infrequent – had I achieved anything for God at all? Had I paid any indemnity?

Something was missing in my life, and I didn't know where to find it. I knew I had had it once.

I seriously contemplated running away again, to California. In California I had been happy. I realised that it was that group of people that had attracted me to the Church initially, and I even wondered what my decision would have been had they belonged to some conspicuously non-Christian group. Though it was a hypothetical speculation, I found it disturbing, for I realised that whatever the California people had believed would have been attractive to some extent, because of the attractiveness of the group as a whole, and the happiness of the community.

At the centre of it all was the need to be loved. That was what I had known in San Francisco, and it was what I seemed to have lost recently in Detroit. Joel's dynamic leadership had given me a sense of belonging, and our team that went to Canada had been a close one. The present leadership, in an attempt to be kind, put no pressure on at all and as a result we had little sense of being bonded together in an urgent and vital task.

When I traced back my three years in the Church, I realised that there had always been somebody I loved deeply. My feelings for Sam in California and Houston, I feel sure, were a very pure, high-minded romantic love, of a type which was encouraged. The possibility of pure friendship was one of the exciting things about the Church. For Jessica and Ruthie at Camp K I had a deep commitment; also for Joel later on, and the team. We were all supporting one another, nobody was backing away from their share of the work. But now in Detroit I was working with some people who would frequently refuse to work and would throw tantrums if things went against their wishes. They were giving way to their Cain-natures, and the leadership had a great deal of trouble with them; certainly they were tolerated in the family rather than loved.

But the people I had loved in California were not there any more. If they were anywhere, they were probably in New York. I prayed fervently that I would be able to go to the workshop. I made a serious effort to transform my attitudes and make my goals. It was hard work, because we were suddenly told that we had to increase our goals, make special conditions, and make a lot of money. We tried to find out why we were being asked to make this special effort, but no information was forthcoming. But it was made very clear that the new goals were to be treated as an absolute priority.

And then one day, when we were in the middle of the new fundraising effort, Mr Fujama said to me, 'I have just had a telephone call from New York. You fly there tonight. You're going on the workshop.'

17 NEW YORK

Reverend Moon has lived and worked in America for several years now. He has been the victim of many slurs concerning money and property. None of the facilities or properties he uses there belong to him personally. They are all legally owned by the Unification Church of America. Even his residence is part of an official centre where international meetings, services and religious ceremonies are held.

[Members of the Unification Church in Great Britain, *The Unification Church: The Struggle of a New Religious Movement*, 1978.]

The foyer of the New Yorker Hotel – owned by the Unification Church – was a vast carpeted expanse. Flowers placed around it only slightly lifted the prevailing air of sombre respectability. Security officers stood conspicuously about, and newcomers were thoroughly checked.

I looked round, somewhat at a loss. An official came over to me:

'Who are you, please? And what is your business?'

It was a very strange feeling to be talked to like that – civilly, but coolly and without interest – in the very heart of the Unification Church. 'I'm Jacqui Williams from Detroit,' I said. 'I'm going on the MFT workshop.'

The guard flipped through a list of names. 'I don't have you,' he said tersely. 'Over there, please.' He pointed to a reception desk.

I trailed across to the desk, and a more friendly face smiled at me. 'Come to the workshop? Right, hold on ...' My name was on her list.

'Fine, that's great. Carry on, Jacqui.'

'Uh – could you tell me what I should do?'

The receptionist shook her head. 'I don't know what the system is from here on in, I'm afraid. I just check names off this list.'

A steady stream of people coming and going passed through the lobby. A man who looked as if he knew his way around entered from the main staircase. I approached him. 'Please, I've come for the MFT workshop and nobody seems to know what's happening.'

He smiled pleasantly. 'Hi. Well, I don't know all that much about the arrangements, I'm just here for a one-off meeting. Say, what family are you with?'

'MFT, Detroit. My name's Jacqui.'

'Glad to know you, Jacqui. Mine's Bill. Now, I happen to know that the MFT people are on the fifteenth floor. Why not go and see them?'

The lift was packed with Koreans, and when it stopped at the fifteenth floor I walked out into a corridor full of even more, laughing and talking animatedly. I began to feel better; this was more like the family atmosphere I'd been expecting. Young children careered up and down the corridor. *I wonder whether Reverend Moon's children are here?* I thought.

There was a room set aside as a waiting room, and I told somebody who I was and sat down to wait. Eventually a girl came in and took my details again. 'I'm Carolyn Schwartz,' she said.

I recognised her name immediately. 'You're the secretary we used to bank-wire our money to from Canada!' I exclaimed. 'I was on Joel Furstein's team.'

'Wow, how good to see you,' said Carolyn. 'Father really

blessed you, didn't he? You were breaking all the records. We were really excited for you. How have things been since your team split up?'

I hesitated. 'I've not been well,' I said. 'I had quite a bad time. And I got rather depressed.'

Carolyn was understanding. 'I hope you'll find this week helpful,' she said. 'Most people do. You'll get to study Principle and discuss and have fellowship, and I think our Heavenly Father has a really great time in store for you.'

Shortly afterwards somebody arrived to take me to my dormitory, which had four beds in it. Then I was introduced to Jan, who was to be my group leader, and the other members of my group.

The workshop was in some ways broadly similar to that at Camp K, but in the afternoons we had to study *Divine Principle* and, literally, sit and learn it. We sat in small groups in corners of the hotel, memorising the passage we were to learn that day.

There was also a very full programme of lectures, and we went fundraising, selling tiny pictures in the Bronx and Queens, two very poor areas of New York. We were not expected to make a great deal of money, but simply to cover the costs of our attendance.

One of the other things we had to do was to go witnessing, something which I didn't look forward to at all after my experience in the Detroit home church. We had to take a chair out on to the sidewalk, stand on it, and address the crowds at the tops of our voices, for five minutes. We all had to do it; I chose as my topic the subject of health foods and people's desire to improve their quality of life. I think I attempted to derive some sort of spiritual application from it, but it was the longest five minutes I could ever recall.

I loved the workshop. Though it was very packed, we had adequate time for sleep, and I developed a friendship with Jan which I really enjoyed. It appeared that she had had some problems herself in her career in the Unification Church, and I was able to talk to her very openly about my negativity and the doubts that I was having.

Jan wasn't a great figure in the Church, but she was a gifted listener. One night, for example, we were talking, and as it grew late she said to me, 'Why don't you come and sleep in my room, so we can carry on talking?' It was, once again, a warm, intimate personal friendship of the sort that I had craved. Here, I felt, was someone I liked, and who understood and cared for me. It was a time of rebuilding, which was fortunate, as none of the Californian people I'd hoped to see were at the workshop.

Others in the workshop were also open and welcoming. An Egyptian man in my group was a particularly good person to talk to, and he helped me a lot. We went fundraising together in the Bronx, and afterwards talked and talked late into the night.

In fact the lectures were less important to me than the friendship. There was an in-depth analysis of world history and the Lord of the Second Advent, and most other aspects of Unification teaching were explored and reaffirmed. But though I worked hard at the lectures and the fundraising, I most of all valued the time I spent with Jan.

And yet once again, there were elements of doubt. Jan, for example, had been matched. She had a husband who had been designated for her, and in due course she would marry him. She wasn't particularly happy about the choice of man, but she had decided to put up with the situation and make the best of it.

I could not say so to Jan, but it seemed to me very strange that the Messiah should choose a husband who really seemed to be wrong for her. I recalled other things I'd been told; that if you genuinely disliked the man that you were matched with, you could decline him and another would be selected for you, and another again if the second one was unacceptable. But surely, I wondered, the Messiah should be able to get it right first time? I added this to my store of worrying things about the Church which I would have to sort out some time.

But against that, the workshop provided a wonderful experience of being part of a much larger unit than I had ever been in in the Church. To sit in the hotel restaurant (which had been converted into a Korean fast-food restaurant), and look about at all the different people, was to realise that the Church was a huge organisation, and that one had a place in it. It wasn't just theory, it wasn't just sixteen-hour days fundraising in unfriendly cities. There were all sorts of people in the Unification Church, including many perfectly ordinary people doing ordinary jobs and living ordinary lives. And that gave a wonderful sense of perspective to my own activities in Detroit.

The workshop came at a crucial point in the history of the church. When I arrived in New York I found out what the reason was for the extra fundraising effort we had been told to make.

Everybody at the workshop was summoned to a special meeting. At that meeting, we were told that Reverend Moon had been issued a writ to appear before the civil courts on charges of tax evasion. He had returned to America from Korea of his own free will to answer and refute the charge. It was up to us, the members of the Unification Church, to establish the right conditions for God to vindicate him. If we were making money, if we were working overtime, if we were making special prayer, fasting, and taking cold showers – then we would be creating a strong foundation for America, so that when the case came to trial, Reverend Moon would be found innocent.

It was, we were told, a parallel situation to that when Jesus stood trial before Pilate, who washed his hands of the matter and passed it on to the civil courts. Reverend Moon's voluntary return from Korea was like a lamb going to the slaughter. And if we, as a Church, did not establish the right conditions before God, then Reverend Moon would have to pay the indemnity for Jesus's trial, and for the sin of the world in accusing the guiltless Jesus. And he would have to pay that indemnity by going to prison.

'America is the most powerful nation in the world,' said the speaker gravely. 'It represents all the nations. And we who love America more than America loves itself, we have a great responsibility.'

There was a reverent silence, broken only by occasional sobs from the group.

The next day we went to hear Reverend Moon speak at a big public rally, and because of the press interest in the case a large audience turned up. A small figure, hard to make out in the glare of the spotlights, he spoke not about his own trial, but on the theme of 'America in God's providence'. It was a speech full of hope. He told the hushed audience that he was not afraid of punishment, that he was innocent of all crimes.

The highlight of the whole workshop came on the Sunday that followed the speech. Every week, lots were drawn in the Church to choose a group of people who would attend Sunday service at the home of Reverend Moon. It was something I knew about and had always envied the New York family for – the chance to spend time close to the Messiah himself. But it was only when I arrived in New York that I realised that all workshop participants were automatically invited.

The journey to Reverend Moon's home was a two-hour drive from New York City. We left the hotel at three in the morning, and before long had left the skyscrapers behind and were driving through the suburbs and finally the open countryside of New York State. All the way I was bubbling with suppressed excitement. I was going to see the man whom I believed to be the Messiah.

The house was flanked by enormous rhododendron bushes, and all around it were ornate gardens. It was a large building built in a gracious age. Our vehicles drew up on the drive and we assembled to go in together.

We all removed our shoes and were shown through high-ceilinged corridors and spacious rooms into a large hall. It was empty. We sat on the floor in rows and said Pledge; then we prayed simultaneously, but quietly, for two or three minutes.

Silence followed. Then behind us a door opened. I did not dare to turn round. Out of the corner of my eye I saw, coming into full view, an attractive Korean woman, wearing a long silk dress. She was leading two children; a girl and a boy. The children looked very neat and tidy.

I recognised Mrs Moon at once from her picture; I'd had several of them in my dormitory in Detroit, and had often gazed at the portrait of the woman who was married to the Messiah. The children, of course, must be the True Children of their marriage. I looked at them in awe.

Mrs Moon and her children waited quietly at the front, heads bowed and hands clasped, Oriental-fashion, in front of them.

Behind, the door opened again and closed gently. Footsteps paced gravely the length of the room. And then Reverend Moon was there, standing with his wife and children; True Parents, in whose name I had prayed so often, and the Perfect Family.

Sun Myung Moon wore a dark suit. I found myself thinking how smart he looked. His hair was much sparser than I had expected. His face was deeply tanned and wreathed in smiles. He seemed the sort of person you could have a conversation with, though his wife remained demure and apart. She had a regal bearing which reminded me of the Queen.

Reverend Moon spoke in Korean, and a translator interpreted. He was an exuberant speaker, and moved constantly. He often bent to cuff the Brothers sitting in the front row, much as Joel used to punch me when he wanted to motivate me.

He was talking about the eye, using it as an illustration of a biblical point. But I could not concentrate on what he was saying. I couldn't take my eyes off him. It was like listening to classical music, when your concentration becomes so finely focused that all reality seems to shrink down to a single point, and everything else disappears. I lost track of time, and took no notice of anything else going on round me. Several times, Reverend Moon looked in my direction, and I felt his gaze penetrating mine. I couldn't believe it. I repeated softly to myself, 'The Messiah is looking right at me.'

He exuded a personal charisma that was almost tangible. Though he spoke in Korean, there was an extraordinary feeling of communication that didn't need words. I was on a spiritual high, intoxicated with the reality of the presence of the True Parents.

And then it was all over. The Perfect Family filed out, and the door closed behind them; and I left with the others, and we emerged into a sunshine that seemed greyer than the room we had left behind.

18 MOVEMENTS

Everyone, without exception, is struggling to gain happiness.

[The Unification Church, *Divine Principle*, 2nd edn, 1973.]

The workshop came to an end, and I returned to my work on MFT. It was almost Christmas. It was, in many ways, a dull period in my life in the Church. The great days of Canada were behind me, and so was the experience of being on Joel's team. Sometimes it seemed as though I were living in the past.

But the present seemed much brighter since the workshop. Up until then I had never met Reverend Moon, and had known of him only through books and lectures. We were told in the Church that we must love Father with all our hearts, and I did love him; but it was only in the sense that I could love anybody whose character and personality I knew second-hand. Until the New York workshop, my love for Father was an intellectual head knowledge, fed by an intense admiration and a devotion born of the fact that I had come to the conclusion that he was the Messiah.

But now I had seen him; I had sat in the same room, I had heard him preach, I had met his gaze. The experience of having seen the Messiah and his perfect family with my own eyes was very precious to me, and I hugged the recollection of every moment of that wonderful day to myself. I thanked

God for making it possible, and I resolved to express my gratitude in a new dedication to the work to which he had called me.

Besides that revelation, I had also had my perspective upon the Church radically enlarged. My life in the Church had so far been lived in small, localised communities or travelling in mobile teams. Almost all of my time was spent talking to strangers who had never heard of the Church before or who had heard of it and disliked it. But in New York I had experienced the impact of the Church as a huge organisation, with members from all parts and thriving like a tree with large and spreading roots.

Being able to talk to Jan had been very important to me. She was the first mature member of the Church with whom I had been able to talk as an equal, rather than as a pupil to a teacher. I realised that many of my problems had been made worse by the lack of people to talk to, and one of the major benefits of the workshop was a certain amount of leisure to think through some of the things that had been troubling me for so long.

I went back on Matthew's team, and though we did not achieve the spectacular results that we had in Canada, we did very well. I regained much of my commitment, and though I was not free of occasional depression, I had many really good fundraising days. When I was 'on centre' and things were going really well, there was nobody I would not approach with my product – I even approached policemen and successfully extracted money from them. On such days I raced from person to person, trying to sell as much product as possible before it was time for my pick-up. It seemed that there was nothing I couldn't achieve, when I was having a good day.

As the New Year receded and the first signs of Spring appeared, I told myself that things were definitely better. I was going to be all right. Even my health was better. Later in the year there would be the Matching, and Father would choose me a husband. It was all going really well. I chanted as I ran the streets, and gave God thanks for the restoration he had given me.

While I was rejoicing in my new-found happiness, firmly convinced that God was removing the final obstacles to a life of full-blooded commitment to the Unification Church, I was quite unaware that on the other side of the Atlantic he was in fact preparing two people who were, in only a few months' time, going to play a very important part in my life.

Donald and Megan Sainsbury lived across the road from my family's home in Windsor until I was fourteen or fifteen. I often looked after their children for them, and I called Megan and Donald auntie and uncle. I knew they were Christians, and I remember very tentatively speaking to them about God when I was a teenager.

They moved out of the area and went to live in Exeter, and I visited them once or twice there. I was awkward and formal with them, because I was making the transition from knowing them as friends of my parents, and getting to know them as my own friends. My friendship with them was longlasting, but it wasn't a very relaxed one.

It was a miracle in their lives that brought them back into touch with my parents. About eighteen months after I went to Camp K, Donald went into hospital for major surgery. Cancer of the bowel had been diagnosed. During that time he received the baptism of the Holy Spirit – for which he had longed for years – in an amazing encounter with God.

Not long afterwards he applied for the post of Chief Executive of Amersham. His application involved a stringent medical examination, which was of course a worrying prospect, and various people in the church were praying that his application would be successful.

The local authority requested a medical report from Donald's surgeon. He was then in his late forties, and in human terms he wasn't a very good prospect. But the surgeon gave him a superb report, despite the fact that he had had a colostomy.

In Exeter they had longed to be part of a church that recognised, and lived its life in, the power of the Holy Spirit; but they had never sensed that God was calling them to move from the church they attended.

But now, because of Donald's new job, it was necessary to move home and look for a local church in Amersham. And that was how they came to discover Amersham Baptist Church. They were thrilled to find that it was exactly the church they had been praying for, and that it had a welcoming, caring congregation.

Returning from their first Sunday service at Amersham, Donald and Megan visited my parents for Sunday lunch. It was a little before Christmas. In America, I was settling back into MFT life after the New York workshop.

They were overflowing with joy at the work of God, and the way he was obviously at work in healing Donald from cancer, getting him the Amersham job, and placing him and Megan in the sort of church which they really longed to be in. They had only just found out that my parents had become Christians, and they were delighted to share with them their discoveries of the power of the Holy Spirit.

They hardly talked about me at all, though they knew I was a member of the Unification Church and were deeply concerned about me. But they knew how painful it was for my parents to discuss it, and they had much to tell them about their new church.

It was the beginning of a renewed friendship between the Sainsburys and my parents, and from that first reunion over Sunday lunch, Mum and Dad had the assurance that there were Christians outside my family who might perhaps be able to minister to me in some way in the future.

In America, the first flush of enthusiasm following the workshop began to fade. Though I never sank into the depths of depression again that I had experienced before the trip to New York, I was aware that my life was still prone to ups and downs.

In a particular sense, the workshop actually contributed to this. In hearing the Unification doctrines of indemnity and human sinfulness taught and re-taught there, I began to develop a sense of guilt which gradually became a backdrop to my whole life in the Church and a spur to greater and greater efforts.

At the workshop and in other ways, we were taught techniques of fundraising that were similar to those used in modern secular salesmanship. We were told to 'accentuate the positive', to transfix our customers with a radiant smile, to fight hard against our human weaknesses and overcome them. Though these techniques worked well, we, unlike salesmen, were not working to build up personal wealth. It was all for other people. The only benefit and motivation for us was a sense of gratitude and acceptance if we made our goals, and the knowledge that we were buying our own redemption and that of our families.

It was motivation enough. But the other side of the coin was that there were days when the best of us felt below par and depressed. Then it was all too easy to lose all regard for ourselves. Certainly, as the years went on, my occasional bad days found me giving in more and more to laziness, wilfulness and selfishness. I didn't care whether I made my goals or not. I lost my self-respect and my self-worth.

There were good days to balance the bad, and the good were very, very good. But on the bad days, I was tormented with such a helpless guilt and remorse for my failure to maintain my progress in the Church that it became harder and harder to climb out of it.

19 ARRESTED

There must be a recognition of original sin.

[Ken Sudo, *120 Day Training Program*, New York, n.d.]

It was just a normal fundraising day down by the Detroit River in late April. Even in the bleak chill of Spring, the city looked as good as it ever had; there was a cold wind sweeping along the streets, and across the grey river waters Canada beckoned temptingly, a distant prospect of city and empty provinces beyond, unusually clear in the wintry air. Nearer at hand the Renaissance Centre towers and high-rise buildings of downtown Detroit looked magnificent.

I was with a girl called Joy, who was somebody I enjoyed being with. She and I had quite a close relationship, and she was a very good fundraiser. We were working the commercial firms on the waterfront.

The smells of the river floated in on the chill air: petrol fumes wafting from a passing cargo vessel, a hint of wood-rot from the debris swirling around the wharf, the transient smells of the empty freight halls, and the heavy scent of the resin used to patch up vehicles in the numerous small auto body shops. And over it all, mournful bleats from ships' hooters and the constant keening of seabirds blended in a tapestry of sound which I'd grown to love.

It was easy to become fond of the waterfront; it was a barren, derelict area with a kind of decaying glamour uniquely its own. Many of the buildings were shells, standing in tracts of rubble, their windows smashed and their roots long rotted, rafters jutting at all angles in a crazy silhouette against the sky. The buildings which were still functional were the huge stone-fronted office blocks in which shipping and other commercial organisations had their offices.

They reminded me of sets out of old gangster films, evoking the vanished world of the 1920s. That impression became even stronger when I went inside the seedy bars which existed in the dim alleyways and shabby streets; often without even a pool table or one-arm bandit as entertainment, they were rough drinking places for rough old men.

But we were not bar-blitzing today. We were after bigger quarry.

'Here we are,' said Joy, adjusting her pack and stamping her feet. 'It'll be good to get into the warm ...'

We were outside the Commercial Rail building, our chief target for the morning. It was a very large organisation which monitored the freight coming through on the rail link from Windsor, across the river in Canada. This was its administration building.

'I'll take the top,' I offered. 'You start with the ground floor. We'll meet up.'

'Right, let's have a look round the back.'

We always avoided entering a building through the front door if we possibly could. In most cases if a receptionist found out that we were selling goods, we would get no further. If all else failed, we would go in by the front entrance, but then we tried to look supremely confident, as if we were going to visit somebody important and would not dream of checking in.

'OK,' said Joy, 'here we go!'

There was a door open at the rear of the building. It seemed to be a staff entrance; a row of lockers stood in the corridor near by. Joy placed her hands on a pipe running along the wall. 'Warmth!' she exclaimed approvingly. 'We'd better get going before we get too comfortable. I reckon the offices will be through there. See you later!' She disappeared down the corridor. I began to climb the stairs.

It went well at first. I was selling our latest product: tin musical boxes, coloured to look like copper. They came in various models and each had a tune appropriate to its shape. They were made in Taiwan, they cost us three dollars and we sold them for anything between twenty and thirty.

I began at the end of a long corridor on the top floor, an old-fashioned, panelled interior with photographs in frames on the walls. I knocked at the first door.

'Come in!'

I pushed open the door. A very fat, middle-aged lady, wearing an unflattering large flower-print dress, was sitting at a solitary desk in a small office. She was drinking coffee; a paper confectionery bag lay crumpled on her desk by her typewriter.

'Hi there, honey, come on in.' She indicated a hard chair. 'What can I do for you? You from Supplies?'

'I'm visiting the offices in this area,' I explained, trying to sound official. 'I have some ornaments I'd like to have you look at. I'm working my way through college by selling goods.' The deceit slipped easily off my tongue.

She looked at me curiously. 'You got clearance at Reception?'

'Oh, right,' I assured her. 'No trouble.'

She gave me a penetrating glance and then giggled. 'Sure, you got clearance.' She giggled again, a high-pitch gasping that made her body quiver. 'No trouble ...' She took a tissue from a drawer and wiped her fingers delicately, one by one. 'OK, honey, show me what you got.'

I demonstrated each model, and she looked at each in turn. 'Play me the aeroplane again,' she said at last. The strains of 'Fly Me To The Moon' tinkled in the office. Through the window, I gazed at the birds wheeling above the river.

'Fair enough.' Her voice, high-pitched and determined, broke into my thoughts. 'I'll have the plane, and the vintage auto – oh, and the Dutch windmill, that's real cute, I'll have that one too. How much?'

I did a rapid calculation. 'Twenty-five each,' I replied.

'Ain't I qualified for a discount? I bought three, didn't I?' Her eyes grimaced in a petulant, demanding frown.

I frowned. 'Let's say twenty each.'

She grunted in satisfaction, and I permitted myself a private smile. Twenty was what I had planned on. Letting her beat me down made her feel good. If I'd been pushed really hard I would have gone to fifteen each to get the sale. 'They're hand-made,' I said generously, to make her feel even better. It was a downright lie, of course, but lying in the course of selling was accepted practice on MFT.

Matters progressed even better; she rang her boss on the internal telephone and he came in and bought two, and soon I was going from office to office doing a roaring trade.

By the time half past five came, I was almost out of music boxes and everybody was preparing to leave for home. The view from the windows showed a slate-grey sky. I decided to move on, and headed down the corridor towards the stairs and the back door.

Coming up the stairs was a uniformed security guard. I stood aside to let him pass, but he stopped when he saw me.

'I've had reports that you're selling things in these premises,' he said. 'I'm going to have to see you out of the door.' He was not unfriendly, but very calm and purposeful. It was a routine annoyance for him.

'Oh! That's fine, sure – I'm going, don't worry.' I had no need to hang around; I'd practically sold out anyway. The guard shook his head:

'You didn't hear what I said. I have to go with you to the

door and personally make sure you go.' He sighed. 'Come on.'

I was flushed with success and felt quite lighthearted; on the way down I chattered about the staff I'd met in the building, and he gave brief and non-committal replies. In the entrance lobby he stopped. 'How long have you been in America?' he asked suddenly.

'How did you know I wasn't an American?' I responded, genuinely puzzled. I'd thought I was quite convincing.

'Your accent, it's British, I can tell.'

'You've got sharp ears,' I said in surprise. 'Not many can.'

'I hear a lot of Canadians,' he explained. 'You get to tell the tiny differences. So how long have you been over here?'

'Oh, a couple of years,' I said off-handedly.

'Do you have your green card?'

His attitude had subtly changed. He was suddenly confident and a little threatening. 'No,' I said. 'I don't carry it with me. Why?'

'You're an alien,' he said. 'You should carry your green card with you at all times.'

'Oh, come on!' I laughed. It didn't seem a great problem. 'You mean I have to have that piece of paper with me everywhere I go?'

'That's just what I mean.' His face was unsmiling. 'And now I'd like to see your passport.'

'Hey, what *is* this?' I protested. 'I haven't got it either, it's at home.'

'Come with me, please.' He wasn't aggressive or harsh; just completely efficient, and inexorable in his attention to detail. I trailed after him to his office.

There were two or three other officials playing cards in the office. They looked up curiously as we came in. I was told to sit down, and he picked up the telephone. I heard him asking to speak to the Immigration Department, and a conversation followed, only part of which I could hear.

I adopted a self-assured, cocky air, and tried to banter with the other guards. They ignored my efforts to start a conversation, and I soon fell silent. In the corridors outside, the last of the employees left for home.

My thoughts turned to Joy and the others. She must have left the building by now and made her way to the pick-up point. I was worried at the prospect of finding my own way back; I had about $400 in my bag, but I would not have dreamed of spending it on a cab home. I would have to walk.

They're taking a long time, I realised. The guard was still at the telephone. Eventually he finished.

'Somebody's coming to see you from Immigration,' he informed me.

'Sure,' I said confidently. Inside, I wasn't afraid. I'd got out of problems like this before. I wondered what kinds of guards they were. 'Do you look after this building? It seems a large force?' I tried to make a joke of it.

'Rail police,' somebody said, but nobody expanded on it.

The Immigration official arrived, a tall man with a drooping moustache and a very relaxed manner. 'You've got problems,' he informed me. 'Your green card is your certification of resident alien status. We can't let you go until we've seen it. Sorry, but we'll have to take you to headquarters.'

'I'm sure it's in order,' I said, though I knew I didn't even have a green card. But I wasn't very worried. It wasn't the first time that I'd had problems. 'Fine, let's go.'

At the front door he paused. A light swirl of snow had begun to fall. People walked past in the street, their coats hunched up over their heads. He looked at my thin trousers and light jacket. 'You going to be all right?'

'Oh, I'll be fine,' I reassured him.

Headquarters, which was like a small police station, was five or six miles away. On the way over I remembered the last time that Immigration and Canada had coincided in my life. *I bluffed my way out of that one*, I reminded myself cynically. *I'll be OK.*

As we went inside, I was shivering. The snow was falling more thickly.

'Like some coffee?' He got me coffee in a plastic mug from a machine in the corner. It was lukewarm, but I gulped it down gratefully. My feet were chilled. The snow was seeping into my walking boots. Usually in bad weather we rubbed bear-grease into our boots or shoes, but this was the first snow for several weeks; it had taken us by surprise. I kicked the boots off and warmed my feet against the radiator.

'Now, what exactly is the situation of your passport?'

I considered telling him the whole story, but decided against it. 'I had to renew it some time ago,' I lied fluently. 'So far as I know, it's all in order.'

'Can anyone bring it here? Where are you living?'

I told them. He waved at the telephone:

'Here, give them a phone call.'

The phone was answered by Joy, who had been back for a while. 'What happened?' she asked.

'I need my passport, I'm at Immigration,' I explained. There was a low whistle at the other end. 'Wow, that's awkward.'

'It's in the loft, in my suitcase,' I continued. 'They're checking my *green card*.' I articulated the words carefully, knowing that Joy would understand.

'We'll send someone out with your passport,' she promised. 'You'll have to make some excuse about the green card.'

By ten o'clock there was no sign of the passport, and there were several crumpled plastic mugs on the table. 'You better ring again,' advised the officer. I did so, and Joy was really surprised. 'We sent the passport ages ago. There must have been problems with the van. We'll get on to it. Don't worry.'

Another officer arrived. He came in covered in snow.

'That weather's a real bitch,' he snorted, flinging off his cape in a flurry of powdery snow. 'Not a flake for weeks then throws it down. Well, what's the problem?'

The first officer explained everything, and then went off duty. His colleague sprawled in a chair and asked me all sorts of questions, in a lazy, humorous way; I told him about the Unification Church, about MFT – I made it sound like charity work – and even a little about *Divine Principle*. He listened patiently. 'I think you should give your friends another phone call,' he said eventually.

Joy was apologetic. 'We just heard, Jacqui – the van broke down. We've got a Brother back here now, he went and found them. He's got your passport. Ask the officer whether he really wants to see it tonight. Mr Fujama thinks you might get away with it. The snow is really piling up.'

The officer listened to my request, rubbing his hands and blowing on them in turn. 'It's a real cold night out there – getting worse. I reckon we'd better call it a day, lady.' He reached for his cape. 'You come in tomorrow with those papers, you hear? OK, I'll run you to the bus station. I want to go home too.'

Outside, the snow stood in drifts against the wheels of his car, and the road was a white blanket; the tracks of cars passing were quickly obliterated by the swirling snowflakes. We drove in a friendly silence to the Greyhound station, where he left me with a final admonition to be at the station the next day.

At the Centre, everybody was delighted at my safe return, and there was great relief. 'We were so worried,' said Mrs Fujama. She looked strained and tired. A very short time after my return I was fast asleep.

Next morning we had a family conference. 'I've been told to go back with my passport and green card,' I told them. 'I don't know what to do. This has happened before and I got round it by moving on – but it would be awfully difficult to do that in Detroit. They took my name last night, they've got all my details.'

'But you haven't got a green card, and your visa's out of date,' Joy pointed out.

'I could bluff it,' I suggested. 'I could say I didn't know that I should have had it all renewed.'

'There is another problem,' said Mr Fujama. 'The Matching in the summer – you are old enough now, and you have been with the family long enough, to be matched. And Father may well match you with an American. So you must have your passport in order, if you are to stay here, maybe even travel abroad.'

'What should I do?'

Mr Fujama sat for a while without speaking, his palms clasped, his head inclined as if in prayer. Nobody spoke; we all waited to hear what he would say. There was a lengthy silence. And then Mr Fujama raised his head.

'Go back to England,' he said flatly.

I looked at him in astonishment. I had expected him to say that I would be moved to another part of America. After all, I'd been caught once trying to get into Canada with my parents, and had got out of trouble by changing my name and moving my base. I'd found that it was easy to lose yourself in America, particularly if you weren't Asian or Mexican or in some other way recognisable as an alien.

'Go to England,' he repeated, 'and get your papers sorted out. See your family. Say your goodbyes. Then come back. We will be waiting for you, Jacqui.' There was an odd note in his voice, almost a threat.

The rest of the team echoed his words in their various ways. 'Come back, Jacqui,' said Joy. 'Don't stay away long. We'll miss you.'

'Don't you worry,' I promised fervently. 'I'll be back.'

Later that day I braved the snow to go to the Immigration Office, where I was told that I had been an illegal immigrant for three and a half years. I registered appropriate shock, dismay and contrition.

'You have a choice,' they explained. 'We can give you what we call Voluntary Departure, where you undertake to leave and we suspend all investigations for thirty days. And then you can apply for another visa back in Britain.'

'And the other option?' I asked cautiously.

'We deport you. And you will find it very difficult to come back.'

'Oh, I'll go back immediately. I'll go on the next plane. I'm just so sorry I've caused all these problems.' I was so successful in portraying myself as an innocent that I left on very good terms with the officials.

Mr Fujama gave me the money for my plane ticket, and some spending money. I packed a few things. Almost before I knew it, I was on a jumbo jet, flying back to England.

20 ENGLAND AGAIN

So aren't you crazy, you young people who are just
blossoming in life, many not even married, yet you are
willing to die for the cause of God! Many people will
point their finger at you and call you crazy and say
Reverend Moon has ruined your life. Even then, are you
determined to go on?

[Sun Myung Moon, *Master Speaks*, August 1st, 1976.]

I had deliberately not told my parents I was coming back to
England. Mr and Mrs Fujama had advised me not to do so.
'Go first to the London centre in Lancaster Gate. Then go to
your parents. Let it be a surprise,' they had said. 'Don't give
them any warning. We have had some Brothers and Sisters
who have been kidnapped by their parents.'

'Perhaps I ought not to visit them at all,' I suggested
doubtfully.

'Oh, no, go and see them – show them how happy you are
doing Father's work, tell them about the Matching, love
them – but don't give them time to make plans. Otherwise it
might occur to them to try to keep you at home by force.'

Mr Fujama smiled, an authoritative, reassuring smile. 'We
would know, Jacqui, we would get word. And we would
find you and bring you home.'

London hadn't changed in four years; if anything, it was
noisier and dirtier than I remembered. I found Lancaster

Gate on a map and made my way there. It was a secluded square off the Bayswater Road, near to Hyde Park. The Centre was in the corner of the square, a building with an imposing entrance portico and the same rather faded high stucco façade as its neighbours. The stateliness of the old buildings made an odd contrast to the noise that filled the square; the central space was occupied by a church covered in scaffolding and apparently being substantially rebuilt.

There were minibuses parked outside the building, and the sight of the vehicles gave me a momentary homesickness for my colleagues on MFT. I pushed open the door of the Centre and found myself in a long, dark hallway. At the end was a small office, where to my delight I found that the receptionist was a girl who had been in California with me. She took me to see Julian, one of the London leaders.

'Well, the first thing we need to do,' Julian said decisively, 'is to get you to see one of our legal people and find out what the passport situation is. You can stay here while we sort it out.' He was very English, well-spoken and well dressed, and rather intimidating.

I was shown to a room on the first floor, where I dumped my things. Later I wandered round the building. It was very different from the Detroit centre – though there was a dining room and a meeting room, it had the feel of an office building. Apart from the receptionist I knew nobody, and hardly anybody I met had time to talk. I felt out-of-place and miserable.

Next day I met the lawyer, and showed him my passport. 'It's been endorsed once already,' I pointed out. During one of my brushes with the law in America, somebody had written on the last page. 'What should I do?'

The lawyer contemplated the ceiling. 'What do *you* think?'

'Maybe I should just lose it,' I suggested. He swivelled his gaze downwards and stared at me non-committally.

I told the Passport Office that I had mislaid it and applied for a replacement. But when they checked my records, they found that I had lost one once before, years ago. The clerk looked at me reprovingly. 'I'm afraid we can't give you another, not just like that. One of the ones you lost might turn up. We *can* give you a replacement passport, but you'll have to wait a few weeks for it to come through.'

Next I went to the American Embassy to apply for a visa, but was told that nobody could see me that day. I decided to wait until my passport came through before trying again.

'What should I do in the meantime?' I asked Julian. 'Should I fundraise?'

'Go home,' he said.

'Not fundraise?'

'No, just go home, spend time with your family. Ring us up if you have any problems. OK?'

I was slightly shocked. It seemed that the British family operated very differently from the American one. Anybody in Detroit finding themselves with time on their hands would have been sent out with a fundraising team.

Somewhat disapprovingly, I followed their advice. I didn't ring home to warn my parents. Explanations would be easier face-to-face.

On the train a confusion of thoughts filled my mind. What would my parents say? I couldn't tell them I had come back to sort out my passport. They thought I had done that after the attempt to get into Canada. Should I just turn up on their doorstep and announce that I was paying a brief visit before going to America to an arranged marriage and a life of service to the Unification Church? I couldn't.

I was suddenly bothered by a burdensome feeling of guilt. All the bad days, all the doubts and agonisings in America had almost crushed me, but at least there had been people there to encourage and challenge me. But now I was on my own, in a train racing towards Windsor and my parents' home, and it all seemed very different.

I could live with lying and deception if it meant furthering the work of God and helping people to come to know the Messiah, but somehow it was a very different matter when it all had to be explained to parents who opposed the whole basis of what you were doing. Was I right to live like that? Were my parents *really* instruments of Satan, trying to destroy my faith?

I arrived in the late evening at the familiar road and walked up to our front door. The house seemed very quiet. It was Easter weekend, and the neighbours seemed to be away from home.

I could see a light in my brother's bedroom window, so I made my way to the back of the house. It looked different from how I remembered it. Then I saw that the house had been altered recently; an extension had been built on to the rear. It was disconcerting, as if it were not my home to which I was returning.

The back door was open, as it always used to be. I went upstairs to my brother's bedroom. Pushing open the door, I found my mother, talking to a girl I didn't recognise.

There were hugs and greetings. 'This is Cathy,' said Mum. 'Stephen's away and Cathy's staying with us for a few days. Why ever didn't you tell us you were coming home? When did you get in? Oh, this is wonderful ...'

Dad appeared, and was equally nonplussed by my sudden arrival. We all trooped downstairs for a cup of tea. With the lights on, I noticed that the house had changed inside as well. There were new furnishings and unfamiliar fabrics. We went into the living room, which I hadn't seen for nearly four years. The new extension had made it larger. I sat down in an armchair which I didn't recognise. Mum was wiping her eyes.

'I wanted to surprise you,' I said lamely. Dad guffawed. 'You certainly did that!'

The next hour was a jumble of explanations and news. I told them all about the flight over, and about Detroit, and how cold it was over there – 'You're hardly dressed for winter,' Mum commented in some concern – and I brought them up to date with all the things that had happened since I had last been in touch with them. Then they shared all their news with me. During the evening a shy fifteen-year old arrived, who was introduced as Simon. Mum and Dad were acting as his foster-parents. I hadn't known about him, and it was a surprise to find a stranger in possession of my bedroom, which was now festooned with heavy metal posters.

It was quite an uneasy homecoming. The most uncomfortable moments were when conversation turned to Sun Myung Moon and the Unification Church, and the sparkle faded from my mother's eyes as I explained that I was only on a brief visit, and had not come home for good. But the awkward moment passed, and there was a great deal of less contentious news to catch up on.

Eventually tiredness overcame us, and a bed was made up for me in Dad's study. I fell asleep partly glad to be with my parents again, and partly disturbed by being unable to sleep in my own room and by the tiny but significant reminders, all over the house, that Mum and Dad were now Christians. *Four years ago I'd have jumped in the air about that*, I pondered drowsily. *So why don't I feel comfortable about it now?*

Next morning my parents went out shopping. I was too tired to go with them, and I sat and talked with Cathy. She was a member of the staff of Scripture Union. Before I left home, my parents would not have dreamed of entertaining a Christian worker out of choice. But Cathy seemed to be on very good terms with them.

She was a very direct person, and spoke frankly. In a way it was a relief. Talking was made easier because I offered to help her wash her hair, which Mum apparently often did. Afterwards I opened up more than I had been able to do with my parents.

'Why did you do it this way?' asked Cathy. 'Coming back so suddenly – not giving any warning – what made you decide to come home like this?'

'It all happened so quickly,' I explained, and told her what had happened over the Immigration papers, and my reluctance to explain things to my parents.

'You haven't got a green card?'

'No, that was the whole problem ... That's what I came home to sort out.'

Cathy looked troubled. 'It seems a lot of untruths to have to tell, to be doing God's work.'

I went on the defensive. 'It's very complicated,' I retorted. 'Out there, it's front line. You'd have to be there to understand.'

Cathy didn't press the point.

Later we sat round the fire and chatted.

'Donald and Megan Sainsbury are back in this area,' said Mum, as she made another pot of tea. 'They're living in Great Missenden.'

'Great,' I said. 'Maybe I'll get a chance to call while I'm over here.' It was as if they belonged to somebody else's life.

'Yes,' said Dad, 'they'd like to see you – why don't you give them a ring while you're home?' He sounded very enthusiastic, which rather put me off, but on the other hand I liked the Sainsburys.

On Easter Sunday I went to a sunrise service down by the river at Windsor, and then went on to the morning service at the church which I had attended before I left for America, and of which my parents were now members – which in itself was a strange situation.

I was greeted with great kindness, but nobody quite knew how to relate to me. Most people tried to talk to me as if I were the same Jacqui they had known before, but were confused when it became apparent that I wasn't.

My looks, too, were a surprise to everybody. I was

extremely overweight from all the fast food I had been eating, my hair was permed, and I wore glasses, which I had not done before. And I spoke with a very strong American accent. Clearly, I was not the same person; and yet people felt that the old Jacqui was there as well, and tried valiantly to make contact.

The feeling of guilt wouldn't go away, even though I told myself it was unjustified. I knew I had changed profoundly, but I was really enjoying seeing my old friends again and didn't want to hurt them. And I was still finding it hard to come to terms with the changes at home, and the fact that both my parents were now actively involved in the church.

I spent some of that week visiting old friends. One was a very old great-aunt of mine whom I visited with Mum and Dad on the Isle of Wight.

Another visit was to London, to Alison, who had been my best friend when I was in the sixth form at school. She had married while I was in America, and I had wished I could have been at the wedding. She and her husband, who attended a local church fellowship and were very happy there, sat and listened as I told them my story. They were good listeners, calm and unthreatening.

One thing that really struck me about them was how deeply in love they were and how easily they communicated. It awoke doubts in me. Later that year I would be married myself. Would I have the same intimacy and friendship that Alison and her husband had? Would my husband even speak the same language as I did? How often would I see him?

I was envious of my hosts. They had something that I could not count on getting for myself. Even deep friendships, such as I had had with Alison, were not long-lived in the Unification Church. Sam and many others had been important in my life and were now out of reach.

God had his hand on my life, of that I was sure. But it was hard to accept that he had so clearly given this couple a

wonderful relationship, when I, whose whole Christian life
was centred on the concept of perfect marriage, seemed
unlikely to experience any of the things which made
marriage meaningful to me at all.

In America I had been buoyed up by the hope that
marriage would be what I had dreamed it would be. In
England, faced with the reality, I wondered whether the
Matching to which I was so much looking forward could
ever come up to my expectations.

I went back to London. 'I'll see you again before I leave,' I
promised my parents, but it was a tearful parting.

At Lancaster Gate I went on a five-day workshop, in
which we studied and memorised *Divine Principle* in the
mornings and delivered lectures based on our studying, and
then for the rest of the day went out on to the streets
witnessing in pairs. There was an evening meal, to which
interested people came, and it was followed by a lecture.

The workshop was quite different in scope from the one
I'd attended in New York, but I found myself comparing
them anyway, to the disadvantage of the London course.
The whole feel of the Lancaster Gate house, too, was
different from our centres in America. It was much more
intense. Nobody sang John Denver songs or entertained
during the evening meal, and members of the Church were
expected to pay for their food. I found it very difficult. But it
felt good to be doing something; after years of non-stop
work, I was not adapting well to leisure.

Yet the experience of witnessing was an unhappy one. I
was frustrated, remembering the ease with which I had
approached people when fundraising and the success I'd
had; witnessing, I had no resources to bridge the gap
between me and the strangers I accosted, and no skills in
persuading them to attend a lecture. Without my product, it
seemed, I was lost.

After the workshop I visited a fundraising centre in

London, where an old friend from Detroit was staying. She too had had trouble with her visa, but because she had a Scottish accent which she had been unable to lose, she had been picked up by the authorities quite easily. She was now working on English MFT, which seemed to be a much less demanding operation altogether than its American counterpart – they even had weekends off.

The English girls, she said, were very excited at the prospect of the summer Matching. Those who were eligible were making wedding dresses and holding themselves in readiness to leave for New York when summoned for the great occasion. I listened to her descriptions of the preparations and was seized by an almost painful longing for America and my friends on the team.

Back at Lancaster Gate I found to my astonishment that Sunday was a regular day off there as well; after morning service we went to Hyde Park to play games and have a picnic.

I spent the next week at the Centre and was kept occupied in study and small jobs, but I dreaded the prospect of killing time at the weekend with people I hardly knew.

I woke early on Saturday morning, dressed and wandered round the building. A few people were already busy at household chores. One or two smiled at me and said 'Good morning'. But I was preoccupied and barely remembered to nod an acknowledgment.

I found myself thinking about Donald and Megan Sainsbury. Perhaps it would be good to see them again. Megan had been a sympathetic listener in the past, and I felt that she would allow me time to tell my story at my own pace. Maybe, if I could get through to just one person like Megan and explain myself, I would be able to get rid of the feeling of guilt and rejection that had dogged me since coming back to England.

There was a telephone near by. On impulse, I picked it up and dialled Megan's number. Drumming my fingers impatiently as the staccato tone drilled down the wires, I glanced at my watch. It was half past seven.

In Great Missenden, Megan Sainsbury was woken by the telephone. She had no idea of the significance of the phone call. It was just an early morning caller wrecking the chance of a weekend lie-in.

'Hi! It's Jacqui!'

Megan glanced at the book lying by her pillow. She'd been reading it late into the previous night: *Chasing the Dragon*, a story of missionary work in Hong Kong's walled city, by a writer called Jackie Pullinger. For a moment her mind raced. *Why ever would ...?* Then she remembered. Jacqui Williams. But the broad American accent hardly sounded like me at all.

'I've just got back from America. I'm in England for a while. Mum and Dad said you were living close by. I wondered, can I come and see you?'

Megan forgot the time and the lazy morning she'd promised herself. 'Oh – Jacqui! I'm sorry I was slow – I'm still half asleep. Yes, please, do come. We'd love to see you.'

Thirty miles away I flipped the pages of a timetable that lay by the phone. 'Uh – there's a train that gets me to you by one o'clock. I'll come on that. Is that OK?'

'I'll be at the station to meet you,' promised Megan.

I packed a few things and left for the station in the mid-morning, still feeling depressed and confused. By now the trauma of the bad times in Houston and MFT had faded from my mind, and my American experiences were stored in my memory as a romantic mix of Californian hillsides, friendly purchasers of product, and joyous times of devotion hurtling along Canadian highways in the MFT van.

And yet, though I was critical of the London family, I was wretched in myself, full of unwelcome guilt feelings and unwanted tensions brought about by my visit home. In my head, I could work it all out. In my heart, I was lonely and upset.

Heavenly Father, I thought resentfully to myself, *take me back to America. There's nothing for me here.*

In Great Missenden, Donald Sainsbury, who also had been woken by my telephone call and had had its contents relayed to him by his wife, was making coffee. Megan was once again at the telephone.

'It's Megan. Look, I've a request for our prayer-chain. Will you pray for a girl called Jacqui? She's coming here this morning. It's a long story ...'

The prayer-chain had only just been set up; this was the first request for prayer that Megan had made. The purpose of the chain was that you asked two or three people to pray for a particular situation, and those two or three people did the same in their turn. It wasn't a gossip chain, it was a network of praying helpers. So even while I was on the train speeding to Great Missenden, there were people praying specifically for me and for my time with Megan and Donald. By the time I arrived, there were a number of people praying.

Turning from the phone, Megan looked at the morning mail. A small package turned out to be a tape cassette. It was sent by a friend in Exeter, and was a recording of a talk given by Jackie Pullinger.

It wasn't a coincidence. *Chasing the Dragon* had made a very deep impression on Megan. Jackie Pullinger describes in the book how, though she was totally inexperienced in the working of the Holy Spirit, she was willing that God should instantly release people from the power and bondage of drugs. She believed that God was saying to her that she would not have to say things over and over again over a long period, but that she would be able to go into the notorious 'Walled City', simply pray with people, and they would be released from drugs and the power of Satan.

The book left Megan with the assurance that, though deliverance from bondage of that sort often has to come about by prayer and faith over a period of time, God can also work instantaneously. The arrival of the tape reinforced this promise in Megan's mind, and she thought about it a great deal while I was travelling to their house. Here she was, totally unprepared and inexperienced in dealing with people who had been involved in strange religious movements – yet God had sent her wonderful confirmation that she would not need expert qualifications for the task he had given her. He would be in control. So Megan, even before I arrived, had complete confidence that God was able, should he choose, to release me instantly from the bondage I was in.

When I arrived at Great Missenden Station, Megan was there to meet me. I recognised her tall, slightly stooped figure waiting by her car. At first she did not recognise me.

'Megan!' I cried. 'It's so good to see you!'

She did not flinch at my thick American accent, but hugged me. Soon we were back at the Sainsburys' large, pleasant house on the edge of a beech wood. We talked and talked. It was the first time I had totally relaxed since arriving back in Britain. Megan and Donald did not betray their astonishment at the change in me, nor did they appear to notice that my voice was pitched stridently loud. They didn't ask about my family or talk about themselves. They asked about me, and sounded genuinely interested and concerned.

Later we went for a long walk through the beech woods. Every now and then I stole a glance at them when they weren't looking, just for the pleasure of seeing them. Megan's hair, framing her deeply tanned face, was beginning to turn grey, and Donald had more of a middle-age spread than I remembered. But as far as I was concerned, they hadn't changed a bit.

After supper, we sat in the drawing room. Megan patted the settee beside her.

'Come and tell us what you've been doing in America,' she said.

It was the first time I had told anybody the story of the past four years. I started with the camp on Lake Huron, and told them everything right up to my departure from Lancaster Gate that morning. Megan and Donald were perfect listeners, asking occasional questions for clarification but allowing me to tell the story in my own way.

'You see fundraising is right at the heart of it,' I explained. 'It's a way whereby people can make an offering. And it's *my* offering also – how hard I work, whether or not I make my spiritual goals. The money is terribly important, Megan. It stands for people's sin.'

The teapot had long since gone cold when I finished. Megan and Donald were deep in thought. Neither of them knew much about the Unification Church. Megan had a leaflet which summarised the main teachings, but they both knew that they had no skilled arguments to counteract anything I might say, nor any special insights into Reverend Moon's theology.

They had prayed that morning that God would take control of the conversation utterly. They knew that God could deliver me from my bondage; but they also knew that he would have to do it entirely by his own power. There was nothing they could contribute. I had not come to the home of two experts in comparative religion.

And yet Megan, in particular, seemed to have a knack of asking questions which were gracious and thoughtful, but which took a great deal of answering:

'I understand, Jacqui ... But as a Christian, how does it make you feel, fundraising?'

I took the question seriously. I appreciated the fact that they had treated me as a Christian throughout and had not embarked on an attack against Reverend Moon. 'Well,' I said slowly, 'when I make my goals – that's wonderful. I really feel I've pleased God.' I paused for a moment, picking my words carefully. 'Then there are some days I don't make my goal, and they're terrible. Missing your goal is just about *the* worst thing that can happen to you.'

In a burst of honesty I added, 'The thing that I find hardest to cope with is that I don't feel all that different whether I'm failing or succeeding. It's not that I'm rebellious or not believing or anything. It's just that some days I succeed and other days I don't. And that's really frustrating, because then I don't know what I have to do to make my goal.'

I felt great freedom in talking with them. I knew they weren't going to interrupt with counter-arguments or shut me up in outrage. And I really wanted to talk. I had no plans to leave the Church, but I did feel that in many ways I was a failure. My visit to England had reopened many of the problems I thought I'd dealt with at the New York workshop, and I was grateful for a friendly audience to help me think it all out.

I told them about the Matching, and why I had come to England. 'I'll probably be engaged later this summer,' I said in a matter-of-fact voice. They must have been shocked, but they gave no indication.

'You were the top fundraiser in America,' said Donald gently. 'Tell me, how did it feel? Did you feel less sinful, more on top of the work when you heard that news?'

I shook my head. 'No ... I had all that success, all those prizes, and next day I had to go out on the streets and start all over again.' For some reason hot tears were pricking my eyes. 'It's like a wheel, Donald. We are so bound by our sin, we can't stop. Father is right. He must be right. All that sin has to be paid for. That's why I'm in America. That's why I'm on MFT.'

I fumbled in the recesses of my memory, and from what seemed years back I remembered a house in New York State and a man who had looked me in the eyes. 'Reverend Moon was born in Korea, that's important, don't you see? It's in the Bible, he will come from the East. He is the Lord of the Second Advent, Megan. He is the Messiah.'

The words fell from my lips and echoed, appallingly, in the air.

Wisely, they left the theological arguments untouched. Neither Donald nor Megan doubted that the central problem was not the theological propositions I was putting forward, but the spiritual attack that I was experiencing. I was caught in a web of spiritual deception. It was no good arguing with me.

But they also believed implicitly that God would deal with the web, the things that were binding me, and that because it was a spiritual deception, it wasn't something that I could deal with myself. God would have to undo it.

It was no brilliant doctrinal analysis which cut away the wall of words I was building, but a gentle question from Megan:

'Jacqui, what does Jesus mean to you?'

I had no answer at all. Jesus meant so much to them, but I couldn't articulate my own theology at all. And it was an intensely personal question.

I felt I was being forced deep into my subconscious thoughts, and that there was something within me that I could not put into words. Having talked almost non-stop for an hour, I now sat silent and embarrassed, unable to say a word. The answers which would normally have sprung to my lips – Jesus weeping at man's betrayal, Jesus having to accept second-best and crucifixion – were ones I knew I just couldn't say to Megan and Donald. They would have seemed irrelevant in that home.

Megan reached for her Bible. 'I'd like to read you some verses from the Epistle to the Romans, Jacqui.' The pages rustled softly as she found the place and began to read: ' "Our old self was crucified with him, so that the body of sin might be done with, that we should no longer be slaves to sin …' "

As she read the verses, it was as if they by-passed my argumentative processes and spoke directly to my heart. I had no desire to resist what was being said to me. I had moved from a world of intellectual argument and rules and regulations, to a situation where I was being ministered to at a much deeper level than mere argument.

Donald broke the silence. 'Megan had a tape sent to her this morning by somebody we've enjoyed. Would you like to hear it with us?'

I said I would, and we moved into Donald's study where the tape player was. I listened to Jackie Pullinger's account of her experiences and the work of the Holy Spirit. Her story struck home in a very direct way. Here was somebody saying 'God did this … God did that …' I was uncomfortably aware that all I had been saying that evening was 'I can't do this … I can't do that …'

The tape came to an end. I was wriggling in my chair, my fingers toying with a medallion I was wearing on a necklace. Finally I took it off.

'Megan,' I asked, 'would you look after this for me.'

She took it in surprise and held it up to the light. The little gold medallion twirled and glittered. She clearly had no idea what it was, but didn't ask.

I didn't volunteer the information; I didn't tell her that what I had removed from my neck was one of the prize medallions I had won for fundraising in Canada.

21 DELIVERANCE

Can a mother forget the baby at her breast and have no
compassion on the child she has borne?
Though she may forget, I will not forget you!
See, I have engraved you on the palms of my hands.

[Isaiah 49:15, 16.]

As I removed the necklace and handed it to Megan, I was
aware that the pattern of thinking which had held me
enthralled for four years was beginning to shift alarmingly.
But I hadn't made any mental decision to leave the Church,
nor had I even contemplated it. The change was taking place
in my heart. The Holy Spirit was dealing with me.

I'd intended to spend the night at my parents' home, but it
was too late to travel, so Megan made up a bed for me in a
spare room, and we all went to bed.

As I lay in the darkened room, a verse which I could not
remember ever having read or heard before came into my
mind. Later I found it in Isaiah 64: 'Your righteousness is
like dirty rags.' The words captured completely how I felt.
I had nothing I could be proud of. I was totally ashamed
of my 'success' as a fundraiser. I knew I was a disaster at
witnessing, but I'd always taken comfort from my fundraising abilities. Now I could hardly bear to think of them.
The doubts and confusions of Detroit fell into sharp
focus.

My own righteousness, my attempts to do good, my efforts to pay indemnity, were all valueless.

I gazed into the darkness, and into my mind came a picture so clear that it was unmistakable.

I could see two giants fighting. As I looked at one of them, he seemed to be the embodiment of rebuke. It was as if his whole being was an accusation to me: 'Reverend Moon is the Messiah. You know he is. If you walk away from him now, you know what that is like? It is like spitting in the face of Jesus. Can you do that? Are you trying to have an easy life? You have forgotten that Jesus said, you must deny all to follow him.'

The other 'giant' locked in combat was my own growing understanding of what Megan and Donald had been showing me. Jesus had paid the price of my redemption on the cross. He had secured my redemption. Only through his death could I have life, and nothing that I could do outside of him could change the quality of other people's lives. Reverend Moon was not the Messiah. I had been drawn into a trap by Satan masquerading as an angel of light.

The vision faded. Bible verses and half-forgotten truths flooded into my mind through the crack which had opened in my heart. The Holy Spirit was bringing them to my memory. In the solitude of that room, the two giants battled it out in my heart.

Both could not be true. If the first was right, then I would have to say to Megan and Donald that I had enjoyed their hospitality but that I believed that what they were saying was wrong. If the other was right, then I had no option but to leave the Unification Church. Either I must deny Jesus, and the lives that Megan and Donald and my parents and Jackie Pullinger were living – or I must deny Reverend Moon.

I struggled for several hours, reviewing the events of the day and the experiences of the past four years. I knew that

God was dealing with me both in my mind and in my heart. I wasn't just working things out in my head. The Holy Spirit was guiding me towards the truth.

Finally, just as I had accepted the teaching of the Unification Church without difficulty, so that night, with God's help, I shook it off cleanly.

It was a bleak acceptance. I was flooded with a sense of remorse. I had grieved my parents, I had mistaken God's will for my life, I'd helped to mislead hundreds of others. I'd abandoned college and all the people who cared for me. *There is no fruit in my life*, I confessed. *In four years I have not changed in any good way. I've messed up.*

And yet, even while the shame was flooding through me, the healing began. I was able to say to God that I really did repent of the past four years. I asked him to give me the power of Jesus Christ's forgiveness in my life, I asked that he would help me to repair all the damage I had done to others and the wounding of my own character, and I asked him to forgive me. Deep inside, I had the knowledge of forgiveness. *This is not the work of any man. I am the God of new beginnings.*

At last I fell into a deep, peaceful sleep.

In the next bedroom, Megan and Donald, who normally slept very well, were having an unusually troubled night. Megan had physical pain, and neither could sleep properly. They recognised it as a sign from God that they should pray; they abandoned any thought of sleep, and together they prayed through the night for me. It was an indication of the battle that was going on in the heavenly places for my release.

Next morning, Karen, Megan's link on the prayer chain, who had been praying for me ever since I arrived, brought some Bible verses. Megan gave them to me when I got up, and one in particular, from Isaiah 44, spoke very directly to me: 'Your sins are like the morning mist.'

In Canada I had once been dropped in Vancouver in the morning, when the city was swathed in mists, and had made my way up some high-rise office blocks. I was in one of them all morning, and when I emerged, the scene around me was staggering. The mists had disappeared, and all around the city were the most beautiful mountains I had ever seen.

Karen's verse spoke to me in just the same way. All the mistakes and wrongdoing of the past four years were swept away like that Canadian mist; and now I could see tremendous vistas of all the wonderful things that God might do with my life. The verse held a wonderful promise for me.

Of course Megan and Donald had no idea yet what had happened. I had arrived at the house as somebody struggling to bear other people's sin; now I was experiencing the power of Jesus to carry my own.

I had handed over the necklace, so Megan knew that God was dealing with me, though she didn't know what was going on inside me. But she and Donald continued praying and sending messages to the prayer-chain to pray for me. I hugged my happiness to myself, biding my time to share it.

That morning we went to church. The worship was a wonderful experience of God's love flowing over me; of knowing his forgiveness and his love for me. I was oblivious to everybody around me. I felt that the sermon was intended directly for me; it was on Ecclesiastes, and the speaker expounded the writer's theme of a world of meaninglessness, such as I had left behind me in America.

By the time we got back to the house, my mind was made up. I had chosen Jesus and rejected Moon; so I wanted to do something, to make a decisive act as a symbol of my decision. Rummaging in my suitcase, I selected a book of sermons by Sun Myung Moon; it was well-thumbed. I had brought it with me to England because it was one I had been particularly fond of. I went into the kitchen; Donald and Megan were in the lounge. A waste-bin stood against the wall. I slipped the book inside.

The only problem left was how to tell Megan and Donald; I desperately wanted to pour out the whole story, but I felt oddly shy, and said very little – though I was aware that my eyes were sparkling and my face kept breaking into smiles. In the end I went upstairs, wrote a note to Megan, and put it on her bed together with all the Unification Church jewellery and literature that I had with me. It was like a small altar of purification, on which I had piled all the tangible remains of the past four years.

Dearest Megan,

I feel that God is asking me to really put on a new nature so I must cast off the old – I just put a book with some of Rev. Moon's words in the bin in the kitchen – I want to ask you to take responsibility for these things – then I can completely put them out of my mind.

The verse Karen sent this morning really touched me –

> 'I have swept away your offences like a cloud,
>   your sins like the morning mist,
> return to me,
>   for I have redeemed you.'

'When you were slaves to sin, you were free from the control of righteousness. What benefit did you reap at that time from the things you are now ashamed of? Those things result in death. But now you have been set free from sin and have become slaves of God, the benefit you reap leads to holiness, and the result is eternal life. For the wages of sin is death, but the gift of God is eternal life in Christ Jesus our Lord' (Rom. 6:20–3).

These things have been my chains – I feel you could give me the key to unlock them. Now I want to step by step take off, shed my chains and bondage to Satan.

Thank you

Jacqui

Megan did not find the note until after lunch. As she read it, she knew that God had freed me. She went straight to the bin, removed the book, and burned it – with hallelujahs! – with the rest of the literature in the garden. The jewellery she flushed down the toilet.

As Megan and Donald read my letter, they were utterly overwhelmed by a tremendous sense of God's goodness. There was great joy in the house that afternoon, when I made the full story known. We rang my parents and told them, and we were all weeping, and in the evening we went to church again and worshipped.

The next day, the elders of the church came to the house. They had not known exactly what was going on, and were very concerned, having heard all sorts of rumours. They arrived thinking that Megan and Donald needed pastoral support in a crisis, but found instead that they were sharing in the celebration of my deliverance.

To involve the leadership of the church, and to set a seal on everything that had happened, the two elders very simply asked me to summarise what had happened. Then they asked me whether I had truly renounced the teaching I had embraced. I replied that I had, absolutely.

They prayed with me and laid hands on me. They asked that I might be filled with, and empowered by, the Holy Spirit; and that Satan would truly and completely be banished.

After the elders had left, we discussed what I should do next. I was expected back at Lancaster Gate at 9.30 the next morning. We prayed about it, and Megan decided to drive me up to London so that I could collect my things and leave a letter for the leaders telling them I would be leaving.

It was a difficult prospect. I did not think that I would be forcibly restrained from leaving, but I was very anxious that the leaders should not see my action as being kidnapped by my parents. I wanted them to know the situation as it really was; that I was leaving of my own volition.

I wrote a letter of about a page and a half explaining why I was leaving, and I included several Bible references. The message went out on the prayer-chain that we were going to the headquarters, and we left with a very strong feeling that we were invading Satan's territory. But we were very confident that God, who had done so much already, would protect us now.

It was almost 9.30 when Megan parked her yellow Polo car in Lancaster Gate. There was only one parking place available, and from it Megan had a good view of the building. She sat in the car and prayed in tongues for the whole time that I was in the building. Neither of us conceded the possibility for a moment that I might be persuaded to change my mind about leaving.

The receptionist whom I'd known in America greeted me with a friendly smile. Julian was coming down the stairs.

'Oh, Jacqui,' he said, 'the meeting's been postponed. See you at ten, right?'

'Uh-huh.' I nodded non-committally, and went to my room.

One of the girls I was sharing with was in the room. 'There's been a room change, Jacqui,' she said. 'You've got to shift your things.'

It was a miracle. It meant that I could carry my belongings through the building without being challenged. Praising God, I gathered up my things quickly. I looked wistfully at a beautiful Korean kimono I had been given by a friend, but I knew that I must get rid of everything that belonged to the past, so I gave it to my room-mate, who loved it.

At the front door as I was leaving, another miracle: the receptionist was nowhere to be seen. So I simply left the letter addressed to Julian on the desk, and took my few possessions out of the building. Blinking in the spring sunlight, I sighed a deep, contented sigh. Across the road, the workmen were busy, pulling down the old church and rebuilding.

Megan started the engine as I appeared. I threw everything on to the back seat and got into the car. We drew away from the kerb. I took a last, fleeting look back.

The Centre looked indistinguishable from its neighbouring buildings: an anonymous façade, its blind windows looking out over the few passers-by in the square. As we turned the corner into the Bayswater Road, the elegant terraces of Lancaster Gate disappeared from view. We joined the flow of traffic moving out of town, and headed for home.

POSTSCRIPT

I will repay you for the years the locusts have eaten . . .
Then you will know that I am in Israel, that I am the
Lord your God, and that there is no other.

[Joel 2:25, 27.]

I never heard anything more from the English family; my
letter was not answered. I had one telephone call from
America, from Mrs Fujama, who rang my parents' house
one weekend when I was staying with them.

'Jacqui, come back,' she said. 'We miss you so much.
Everything is forgiven. You must come back for the
Matching. Father desires that you should be Blessed.'

As it happened, I had posted a letter to her a few days
before, explaining what had happened. 'Mrs Fujama,' I
said, 'I can't talk on the telephone for very long, but there
is a letter on its way. I don't think I will be coming back.
Thank you for your love to me.'

She became angry, then as quickly began to weep. My
heart was racing. I was very fond of her, and we had been
very close. But I know new that she had no power over
me at all, and that I was finally free.

Going back to Lancaster Gate had been a very important
experience for me. I had been into Satan's stronghold,
and the Holy Spirit had gone before me. He had prepared
Julian to meet me on the stairs, the girl in the room to tell

me about the room change, Megan's parking place, everything.

It was a picture of what God had done in my life for the
past four years and long before. Nothing that I had done or
learned in the Unification Church had happened without
his knowledge. There was no time when I was out of his
sight or out of his love. And when the time came that he had
chosen for me to be delivered, he did not use deprogrammers, or skilled counsellors, or theological scholars – valid
though each of these might be in some circumstances;
he used people who were fearful of their own lack of
knowledge and strength, and turned to him for help. I was
delivered from my bondage by the strong arm of God
himself, and the glory and honour for that belong to no
other.

I left the Unification Church in 1982. I was twenty-three
years old. I had been a member from the age of nineteen.
Four of the most formative years of my life were thus
written off completely. They left no legacy: no friendships,
no money, no possessions, no professional training; only
commercial skills I would not care to use in the real, 'outside'
world. Not only did I leave the Unification Church with no
ticket for life, but on entering that cloistered community I
had severed all past ties. Only those people who were truly
committed to me remained.

Donald and Megan Sainsbury quickly absorbed me into
their home and the extended family of their church, and
during the six months that followed, I began to relax. I
learned how to sleep for more than four hours at a time. I
began to eat regular, healthy meals. And, most important of
all, I started to talk.

Megan and I walked for hours in the peaceful Bucking-
hamshire countryside as I poured everything out to her. I
probed the recesses of my consciousness, finding new
references and perspectives for understanding what had

happened to me, and what unsatisfied needs in me had made the Unification Church seem so attractive. After hours and days of talking, we unearthed that most basic of needs; the need to belong. I had wanted to belong to someone and to some group of people; but I had had high expectations of both.

Perhaps I had thought that in Sam I had met a man who possessed the qualities I was looking for, albeit subconsciously. The more I probed him the more sound and attractive his credentials had seemed. The environment in which we had lived had been like an ivory tower, and there had been little to boost my flagging confidence and low self-esteem. Sam's obvious interest in me as a person, and his total sincerity, had been very disarming.

Through hours of painfully honest self-analysis, identifying past hopes and fears, I discovered the release of sharing one's real self openly with another person, and the reality and hope which God gives. I began to build up the beginnings of a vision that there might be a future; the past, despite my weaknesses, was evidence of God's faithfulness.

I came to understand that the values and ideals I had had before I joined the Unification Church had been like idols. In my heart I had broken the second commandment: 'You shall have no gods before me' (Exodus 20:3). Jesus said that the greatest commandment of all was to 'love the Lord your God with all your heart, with all your soul and with all your mind' (Matthew 22:37). I had not loved him like that, which was why I was able to be deceived into loving Sun Myung Moon.

During those months I read Exodus and Deuteronomy. I came to see my years in America as a period like Israel's captivity in Egypt; a period of my life of which I could never be proud, but which was used by God in a wonderful way to display his sovereign power and his deep and intimate love for me. As I immersed myself in the Bible, I received the assurance that the lost years – 'the years which the locust had eaten' – would be restored, and the loss would be turned into gain.

Though I left the Unification Church empty-handed, I did not leave as a bitter and angry victim. I left as a free woman, still mindful of those I had left behind. As I took the first steps into my new life, I thought often of those who were still inside the Church.

In my experience, Moonies are not coerced or manipulated by some human agency. They are in subjection to a set of teachings, and a leader who is himself deceived into following a hollow and meaningless philosophy.

One of the most damaging aspects of Unification doctrine is the way it purports to build upon the Judaeo-Christian tradition by making passing references to the Bible. Single verses are usually quoted out of context and reinterpreted according to a whole new system of symbolic and allegorical meanings outlined in *Divine Principle*.

Unification theology reflects a variety of influences: Eastern mysticism, scientific terminology, Taoism, numerology, anti-Communism and Moon's own revelations. It is all presented in a well-researched, logical framework. Yet when it is closely analysed it denies the central point of all human history: 'This is how God showed his love amongst us: He sent his one and only Son into the world that we might live through him. This is love: not that we loved God, but that he loved us and sent his Son as an atoning sacrifice for our sins' (1 John 4:9,10).

As I began to read the Bible with new enthusiasm, it was as if I read it for the first time. I saw clearly how the New Testament proclaimed Jesus's place as the fulfilment of prophecy, and how urgently it warns against those teachings that can insidiously lead even the faithful into error.

The character and lifestyle of the average Moonie, I know from my own experiences, can vary greatly from one country to another. The most recent mass weddings transformed the movement in the West. Most members are now married and are producing families. The rigorous travelling life has, for the most part, been replaced by longer-term missions.

The Unification Church is constantly investing resources in improving its public image. During Sun Myung Moon's imprisonment for tax evasion in America in 1985, the Church undertook a massive literature campaign. Packs containing *Divine Principle* and a book of Moon's teachings, together with videos promoting Unification teaching, were sent to 300,000 American churches. This illustrates the extreme lengths to which the Unification Church is prepared to go to present itself to the Christian Church as intellectually, morally and doctrinally viable – an authentic Christian denomination.

Because of this shift in emphasis, chance encounters with Moonies selling house-plants door-to-door, or distributing literature outside Underground stations or on university campuses, are not very common in Britain. Nevertheless, I am sometimes asked how best to respond to such an approach.

My story reveals fundraising to be a depressing and strenuous activity. Looking back, one of the saddest aspects of my time on MFT was the fact that on several occasions I was confronted by Christians who seemed to be hard-hearted and self-righteous. They were only interested in accusing me, threatening me with a vengeful God, and slandering Sun Myung Moon. Few asked my name or took any interest whatsoever in me as a person.

And yet I am convinced that when I left, it was because I was 'prayed out' of the Unification Church by people who loved me and trusted God for my future. That is why I do not believe that professional deprogrammers who demand vast sums of money to pull people out of the

Unification Church can ever be truly successful. Where
they gain their objective they do so by intimidation, force,
coercion and emotional leverage. Unification Church members are trained to resist arguments; but nobody can resist
love.

After several weeks of rest and rehabilitation, I gained
enough confidence to resume my studies. I was accepted at a
local college, and completed my training as a teacher. I now
teach in a primary school, and my job is a stimulating and
very enjoyable challenge.

With the resumption of a regular lifestyle, my health
improved. I lost weight and regained energy. My speech
gradually lost its strident edge and harsh drawl. The mystery
of my illness while on MFT was resolved when, not long
after coming home, I was successfully treated for gall-
bladder problems – almost certainly a legacy of many hastily
eaten convenience-food meals, lack of sleep and constant
pressure. My stomach cramps in America were probably the
first signs.

Today, I am part of a large, vibrant and growing family
of Christians in Bracknell, Berkshire. Visitors are welcomed with the verse 'Come unto us and we will do you
good' (Numbers 10:29). Our elders have a teaching
ministry that takes them all over Britain and abroad, and
the church is full of ordinary, everyday people whose
lives have been dramatically touched by the power of
the Holy Spirit and who are experiencing a living relationship with God through Jesus Christ. In that church I
have found friendship, acceptance and support, and the
opportunity to worship and grow in faith alongside
others.

My years in the Unification Church have not blighted my
life for ever. I do not live under a dark shadow. God has in
truth given me back the years that the locust had eaten. In the
first weeks after leaving, I wrote a song, based on words

from Joel and Isaiah. It was an expression of my response to God's great love and faithfulness.

The Locust Song

(To the tune of 'O Waly Waly';
sometimes sung to 'When I Survey, the Wondrous Cross')

O never leave the Lord your God,
Lean not upon your own understanding,
Do not be wise in your own eyes;
Trust in the Lord with all your heart.

And all the years the locust has eaten
I will restore, I will restore,
The threshing-floors shall be full of grain,
You shall eat in plenty and be satisfied.

I will comfort all my children who mourn,
And bestow on them a garland of beauty
The oil of gladness, a garment of praise,
A double portion for their inheritance.

I will pour out my spirit on all mankind,
Your sons and daughters shall prophesy,
Old men dream dreams, young men see visions,
And Jesus shall be glorified.

*   *   *

Jacqui Williams can be contacted care of Ben Davies:
Bracknell Baptist Church
Church Road
Bracknell, Berkshire.